Jesus Christ and the
Origin of Christianity

Jesus Christ and the Origin of Christianity

R. D. Rucker, Ph.D.

VANTAGE PRESS
New York

FIRST EDITION

Published by Vantage Press, Inc.
516 West 34th Street, New York, New York 10001

Manufactured in the United States of America
ISBN: 0-533-10323-1

Library of Congress Catalog Card No.: 92-90793

0 9 8 7 6 5 4 3 2 1

To the memory of my paternal grandparents, Eli Rucker and Emma Finch, and my maternal grandparents, Noah Tidwell and Florence Tompkins Rowland (March 16, 1879–December 26, 1990), and my step-grandfather Waymon Rowland

Contents

Preface

More than Peter, Paul, Matthew, Mark, Luke, and John, and more than any of his disciples, Jesus of Nazareth shaped Christianity into a movement that eventually ushered in a new era in world history.

While before his trial he had not urged recruitment of Gentiles, the victory of the Jewish ecclesiastical establishment in Jerusalem over Jesus and his followers compelled his disciples to branch out from Israel to save more than the Jews. In the process, of course, they saved Christianity and made it a world religion.

The evidence establishes that Christianity began at the moment John the Baptist baptized Jesus. Its conquest of Europe commenced, however, from the moment Jesus died there on the cross in Jerusalem.

My study explains why Jesus failed. But it also reveals why, and it shows in what way, he succeeded. It makes clear what Christianity is, delineates what Jesus did, and establishes who he happened to be.

Jesus Christ and the
Origin of Christianity

Chapter 1
Birth

Surprisingly, we know so much about the early years in the life of Jesus of Nazareth. He was called the Messiah or the Christ, the one anointed by God. We know him simply as Jesus Christ.

It is clear that Jesus was Jewish. While, in due course, we shall see what else this meant, basically it meant that he was a descendant of Abraham. In fact, he could trace his ancestry from Mary, his mother, to Abraham.[1] Mary was Jacob's daughter.[2] Jacob was Joseph's father-in-law.[3] And Joseph is Heli's son.[4]

While we do not know whether Jesus ever met his maternal grandfather, it is clear that his lineage went back forty-two generations. Jesus was twenty-eight generations removed from Israel's greatest king.[5] And as David's heir, he was called "the son of David."[6]

On his father's side, Jesus' bloodline is unknown. This is because we know only of his legal father. Besides God, his ultimate father, Jesus knew only his stepfather, Joseph. Through his stepfather, the father who reared him, Jesus could trace his ancestry to King David because Joseph, like Mary, was of the Davidic line.[7] By his name and house, Joseph was called "Joseph, son of David."[8] Legally then, as also by blood, Jesus was heir to the throne of Israel. If Israel would have had a king, Jesus would have been literally, as heir apparent to the throne, King of the Jews.[9]

There is something else extremely significant about the descent of Jesus through, in a legal sense, Joseph. Joseph could trace his ancestry back to Abraham and beyond Abraham to Adam, the

1

first man according to Jewish biblical tradition. Moreover, according to that tradition, Adam was one of the primary creations of God, that is, the "son of God."[10]

Jesus could trace his lineage, then, from Joseph to God. In the Christian tradition, he is no mere carpenter's son. He is the Word of God[11] because Joseph could trace his ancestry back to God and because, as Joseph remembered it, God commanded him to adopt Jesus.[12]

Besides his lineage through Joseph, something else, however, caused Jesus to believe himself to be God's son. This involved what happened, or what he was told happened, at his conception and before his birth.

Mary had been "engaged" to Joseph.[13] She lived with her parents because, as Luke tells us, after visiting the mother of John the Baptist, she "returned to her home."[14] While betrothed to Joseph, but "before they lived together, she was found to be with child from the Holy Spirit."[15] In other words, Joseph was not Jesus' biological father. He was, however, under Jewish law and by God's command, Jesus' legal father because he adopted Jesus and named him.[16]

Joseph eventually "found" Mary "to be with child," that is, to be pregnant.[17] Understandably, he became upset and was extremely disappointed. After all, Mary was supposed to become his wife. Being a "righteous man and unwilling to expose her to public disgrace," he planned simply "to dismiss her quietly."[18]

Jewish law suggested the propriety of this plan. Under Jewish law, "If there is a young woman, a virgin already engaged to be married, and a man meets her in the town and lies with her, you shall bring both of them to the gate of that town and stone them to death, the young woman because she did not cry for help in the town and the man because he violated his neighbor's wife."[19] Thus, pursuant to Jewish law and if she could not otherwise prove that she had not slept with a man, Mary faced death by stoning.

Joseph resolved, therefore, to dismiss Mary without revealing

2

her pregnancy to the people of Nazareth. But as he did not want to be precipitous in his action, he would think on it through the night. As he slept, however, he had a dream.

In the dream, an angel, one of the angels said to serve the Lord,[20] appeared to him. What the Lord's angel told Joseph changed his mind. On awaking, Joseph remembered the dream and the angel's message:[21] "Joseph, son of David, do not be afraid to take Mary as your wife, for the child conceived in her is from the Holy Spirit. She will bear a son, and you are to name him Jesus, for he will save his people from their sins."[22]

Joseph followed this plan. He took Mary "as his wife, but had no marital relations with her" until after she had given birth to her baby.[23] As her husband, and because he adopted the boy as his own son, Joseph "named him Jesus."[24]

Jesus, therefore, was conceived through the Holy Spirit or the power of the Most High.[25] That, however, is by no means so unusual. All humans are born this way. Whoever are our parents, they are only the medium through which we are born. Life is ever continued, but only once created.[26] We are of our parents because they produce us. They produce us because by our birth, nature perpetuates the human species.

Mary knew, more than Joseph, how Jesus was conceived. She told her story to some of the disciples. She also seems to have told the story to Joseph because Joseph learned from her that she was supposed to be "with child from the Holy Spirit."[27]

Joseph could not take this story seriously. And he would not have taken it seriously except for what happened in his dream at the very moment he formed his inclination to dismiss her.

Both Joseph and Mary lived in Nazareth, a town in Galilee in northern Palestine.[28] Mary had relatives who lived in the hill country in a town of southern Palestine. Elizabeth, who lived there, "was said to be barren."[29] Zechariah, a priest and Elizabeth's husband, was an "old" man. From the point of view of biologically having children, Elizabeth was "getting on in years."[30]

Zechariah's prayer had long been for a son.[31] About fifteen months before the birth of Jesus Christ, and while in the sanctuary, Zechariah had a vision.[32] He foresaw that his wife, Elizabeth, would become pregnant. And they would name the baby, a boy, John. John would become a prophet. His special mission would be to "make ready a people prepared for" the Messiah.[33]

The news of Elizabeth's pregnancy reached Mary in Nazareth moments after she had been informed through a dream by the angel Gabriel that she herself would bear a son.[34] Mary deemed herself to be a servant of the Lord. And what God said, she believed.[35] The *thought* of becoming pregnant occurred to Mary, therefore, she revealed, before her pregnancy. Previous to the conception of Jesus, as John put it, there was the Word.[36]

Jesus was born during "the days of King Herod of Judea."[37] Necessarily, then, he had to have been born at some point before the death of Herod, the King of Judea, in 4 B.C.

We know that Jesus was born during the life of John the Baptist because he was conceived during the sixth month of Elizabeth's pregnancy.[38] Mary believed that the Holy Spirit came upon her and "the power of the Most High" protected and "overshadowed" her[39] because she, and the fetus within her, escaped death under Jewish law.

Mary could take no chance however. She decided it best to leave Nazareth for Elizabeth's.[40] She set out in haste. Eventually, on her return from the hill country three months later,[41] the Most High took, or is believed by Mary to have taken, an important step to protect her. An angel, and presumably Gabriel, was sent to change Joseph's mind about ending the engagement. As a result, although learning from Mary of her pregnancy, Joseph took her as his wife. At least three years would pass before they would return to Galilee since, before the birth of Jesus but while Mary was pregnant, Joseph and Mary traveled to Bethlehem, a town in Judea.[42]

4

Chapter 2
Childhood

From data supplied by Mary, New Testament authors revealed the approximate moment Jesus was born. "In those days a decree went out from Emperor Augustus that all the world should be registered. This was the first registration and was taken while Quirinius was governor of Syria."[1] Thus, Christ was born while Augustus Caesar (63 B.C.–A.D. 14) was emperor (27 B.C.–A.D. 14). Caesar's decree required all inhabitants in the provinces to go "to their own towns to be registered."[2] Accompanied by Mary, "Joseph also went from the town of Nazareth in Galilee to Judea, to the city of David called Bethlehem, because he was descended from the house and family of David."[3]

Although abstaining from sexual intercourse with Mary, because she was then in her late pregnancy, Joseph resolved to marry her in accordance with his vision. He eventually "took her as his wife."[4] This should not be taken to mean, however, that Joseph married Mary before the birth of Jesus.

The evidence seems to compel another conclusion: Joseph and Mary married in Bethlehem because Joseph "had no marital relations with [Mary] until she had borne a son."[5] Other evidence substantiates this interpretation: "[Joseph] went to be registered with Mary, to whom he was engaged and who was expecting a child."[6] Thus as he and Mary went to Bethlehem, he was not then married to Mary. While in Bethlehem, Mary gave birth to Jesus and married Joseph.[7]

5

Some scholars assume necessarily that biblical sources are in error about the birth of Jesus in Bethlehem.[8] As the information must have come from the boy's mother, there is no reason to doubt the account. "And she gave birth to her firstborn son and wrapped him in bands of cloth, and laid him in the manger, because there was no place for him in the inn."[9] In other words, Jesus was born in a stable. Placing him in the hay of the manger appears to have been quite reasonable.

While Rome's decree is said to have provided the occasion, Joseph might have had another reason for leaving Nazareth. Just as people gossip in small towns all over the world, Jews talked in small town Nazareth. By their traveling to Bethlehem, Joseph knew that there would be less talk in Nazareth about Mary's pregnancy. Since she was traveling with him, no one would question that she was bearing his son.

By naming the boy, Joseph adopted him as his own son. As the "husband of Mary, of whom Jesus was born," Joseph became Jesus' stepfather and his legal father.[10] Joseph and Mary lived together as husband and wife and had "marital relations," that is, among other things, sexual intercourse.[11] Proof of the fact is not left to surmise.

Matthew and Luke both make clear that Jesus was not the exclusive child born to this marriage. While in Bethlehem, Mary gave birth "to her **firstborn** son."[12] Thus, by implication, Mary gave birth to more than one son. Matthew confirms, in fact, that at one time Jesus' mother and his "brothers" came to visit him. Someone told him, "Look, your mother and your brothers are standing outside, wanting to speak to you."[13] We can conclude then that Jesus had brothers. Some evidence suggests that he had a sister and/or several sisters.[14] His family consisted therefore of his legal father, his biological mother, his brothers, and his sisters. His maternal grandparents, or one of them, alone with his mother's sister, lived near them in Nazareth.[15] His mother's relatives,

6

Zechariah and Elizabeth, with their son, John, lived about a day's walk from Nazareth in the hill country of Judea.[16]

As every loving mother hopes her son will turn out to be, Mary had reason to believe that her son would be someone special. Even before his birth, but while Mary was pregnant, Elizabeth had suggested that Mary's baby would turn out to be the "Lord."[17] Zechariah asserted in fact that the Almighty had "raised up a mighty savior for us."[18] John's parents thought that Jesus would become the Messiah. John would become, in turn, "the prophet of the Most High," going "before the Lord to prepare his ways."[19]

Something else beside Zechariah and Elizabeth's attitude confirmed to Mary that her dream had been no idle vision. Some shepherds were working in the fields on the night Jesus was born. They seemed to see an angel. The angel explained that the Most High had sent them the gospel. The "good news" was that there was born that day in Bethlehem "a Savior, who is the Messiah, the Lord."[20] The shepherds went therefore in haste and found "Mary and Joseph, and the child lying in the manger" in Bethlehem. They told Mary and Joseph that an angel had appeared before them and announced that Jesus would be "the Messiah, the Lord."[21] Mary was quite amazed. "But Mary treasured all these words and pondered them in her heart."[22]

Joseph and Mary were married and then, before eight days passed, someone came and circumcised Jesus in accordance with the practice of the Jews.[23] The boy cried. The foreskin had been cut from his penis. He was being brought up Jewish.

About two years after his birth in Bethlehem, some astrologers came "from the East" to Jerusalem.[24] These "wise men" had studied the heavens and had traveled from Iran and/or Ethiopia. In their view, the configuration of the stars meant that something wonderful had occurred in Jerusalem: that, as they reasoned, a king had been born to rule over the Jews. The "wise men" therefore traveled to Jerusalem. Once there, they asked: "Where is the child who has been born king of the Jews? For we observed his star at its rising, and have come to pay him homage."[25]

Apparently the star had appeared earlier, even as much as two years earlier.[26] We know from Matthew that the wise men did not visit Joseph and Mary while, as commonly believed, their son slept there in the manger. Matthew tells us that by the time the wise men reached Bethlehem, the Jesus family was living in a house.[27]

We can conclude then that the wise men did not visit a baby. They called on a two-year-old boy.[28] And he was not in a manger, but in his parents' home in Bethlehem. "On entering the house, they saw the child with Mary his mother; and they knelt down and paid him homage."[29]

Tradition has it that there were three wise men. All the proof seems to substantiate the traditional view. Matthew tells us that the wise men opened "their treasure chests."[30] This seems to imply that each had valuable property. From these treasure chests, "they **offered him** gifts."[31] By implication then, there were three wise men and each presented a gift. One gave gold. Another gave frankincense. And the third gave myrrh. It is significant that they did not give these gifts to Mary for the boy.

The gold, frankincense, and myrrh were, like money, a medium of exchange. It soon became clear to the Jesus family that the treasures offered were extremely valuable. If they were not from the treasury of the Most High, they were definitely miraculous gifts.

The wise men knew that someone was born and born King of the Jews. Necessarily, in Jewish biblical tradition, a Jewish king, because born in the Davidic line, had to be born in Bethlehem. The wise men deemed the child to have already been born. Moreover, they said, he was born heir-apparent to the Jewish throne. They had observed his star in Iran and/or Ethiopia "at its rising."[32] Its setting seems to have led them to Bethlehem.

A Jewish king on the throne in Jerusalem would be, however, a sure threat to Herod. "When king Herod heard this, he was frightened, and all Jerusalem with him."[33] Herod seems to have thought it meant the overthrow of his government. He therefore aimed to find, and then to destroy, the heir-apparent to the throne of Israel. "[C]alling together all the chief priests and scribes of the people, he inquired of them where the Messiah was to be born."[34] The Jerusalem ecclesiastical establishment explained where, according to Judaic tradition, the Messiah was to be born. " '[F]rom you [Bethlehem] shall come a ruler who is to shepherd my people Israel.' "[35]

On learning of the birth of the heir-apparent and that the heir to the Jewish throne supposedly was to be born in Bethlehem, Herod sought to use the wise men against Jesus. After paying homage to Jesus in Bethlehem, however, all of the wise men, or at least one of them, had a vision during a dream. They came to see that Herod sought to locate the Jesus family to harm the boy rather than pay him homage. The wise men, therefore, proved themselves sagacious. They left for their country in the East without returning to Jerusalem.[36]

Up to the visit of the wise men, Mary, Joseph, and the boy Jesus faced no danger in Jerusalem. They went there frequently. Luke tells us, in fact, that, "When the time came for their purification according to the law of Moses, they brought him to Jerusalem to present him to the Lord."[37] Mary carried a pigeon or a turtledove to the temple priest for a sin offering. But she did that when "the days of her purification [had been] completed," that is, thirty-three days from the boy's birth.[38] This supports our thesis, then, that the wise men did not visit Jesus at his birth. The Jesus family would not have gone to Jerusalem had the wise men visited and Joseph had learned of Herod's threat.

We know, therefore, that in the second month after his birth, Jesus made his first appearance in Jerusalem. Mary and Joseph entered the temple with Jesus.[39] Something extraordinary then happened. An old, devout, and righteous man, called Simeon, took **baby** Jesus into his arms. Although she may not have known its

9

meaning, Mary remembered through all the days of her life what Simeon said as he held baby Jesus:

> Master, now you are dismissing your servant in peace, according to your word [Simeon was not supposed to see death until he had seen the Messiah]; for my eyes have seen your salvation, which you have prepared in the presence of all peoples, a light for revelation to the Gentiles and for glory to your people Israel.[40]

Old Man Simeon revealed therefore that as the Messiah, Jesus would bring honor to the Jews because he was Jewish by birth. However, as things would turn out, Jesus would succeed primarily in being "a light for revelation to the Gentiles."[41]

Mary was struck with amazement.[42] Simeon then told Mary explicitly, "This child is destined for the falling and the rising of many in Israel, and to be a sign that will be opposed so that the inner thoughts of many will be revealed—and a sword will pierce your own soul too."[43] Whatever Simeon was telling Mary, he confirmed her belief that Jesus was fated to do something great. But, as he rose greatly, Simeon noted that Mary herself would come to grief.

At about this moment, an eighty-four-year-old woman, Anna, approached Joseph and Mary in the temple and began announcing to all that they could and would find salvation through Jesus.[44]

Luke tells us what Joseph and Mary did next. "When they had finished everything required by the law of the Lord, they returned to Galilee, to their own town of Nazareth."[45] While true, that was not the whole story.

We know that upon leaving the temple Joseph and Mary returned to Bethlehem and lived there in a house until after the visit by the wise men. "Now after [the wise men] had left, an angel of the Lord appeared to Joseph in a dream."[46] The wise men had warned Mary and Joseph to be careful because Herod had less than a benevolent attitude toward the birth of a new king. Joseph thought about it, and he went to sleep. He dreamed that an angel of the Lord appeared to him, saying, "Get up, take the child and his mother, and flee to Egypt, and remain there until I tell you; for Herod is about to search for the child, to destroy him."[47]

Thus, to escape Herod's wrath, Joseph set out for Egypt with Mary and Jesus in the middle of the night. There was, however, another reason for Joseph to go with Mary and Jesus to Egypt. Through the prophet, as Joseph knew, the Most High was to have said, " 'Out of Egypt I have called my son.' "[48] Joseph therefore left for Egypt and remained there until in a dream, as Joseph expressed it, he had been told by the Most High that it was safe to return to Palestine.[49]

On learning that he had been tricked by the wise men, Herod became furious. He would find the boy Jesus and exterminate him. His decree ordered the death of "all the children in and around Bethlehem who were two years old or under, according to the time that he had learned from the wise men."[50] Although he succeeded in murdering all such children, he never found, of course, the Jesus family, and he soon died.

At Herod's death, as Joseph recalled it, an angel of the Lord appeared to him in his dream and said, "Get up, take the child and his mother, and go to the land of Israel, for those who were seeking the child's life are dead."[51]

Joseph had planned to return to his house in Bethlehem. But, as Herod's son, Archelaus, now ruled Judea, Joseph thought it unwise. Moreover, in another of his dreams, as Joseph recalled it, an angel of the Lord warned him to avoid Bethlehem. The Jesus family, therefore, returned to their former hometown.[52] "There [in Galilee, Joseph] made his home in a town called Nazareth."[53] Jesus' growing up in Nazareth meant that, indeed, he would "be called a Nazorean."[54]

Chapter 3
Youth

Shortly after the death of Herod in 4 B.C., Joseph, Mary, and the boy Jesus terminated their stay in Egypt. "When they had finished everything required by the law of the Lord, they returned to Galilee, to their own town of Nazareth."[1]

The best available evidence suggests, therefore, that Jesus was three years old at the moment he arrived in Nazareth. We are dating, therefore, the birth of Jesus from approximately the winter of, or on or about December 25, 6 B.C.[2]

Joseph, Mary, and the boy Jesus seem to have visited the temple in Jerusalem annually "for the festival of the Passover."[3] Jesus grew from a three-year-old boy into a young man. He became "filled with wisdom."[4] He learned to read and to write in his native Aramaic language and in Hebrew. He studied the Old Testament. He became skilled in debate, proficient in the Mosaic law, and perspicacious in his understanding of the word of God.

One of Jesus' salient visits to Jerusalem occurred "when he was twelve years old."[5] Mary remembered the visit many years later.[6] She recalled something extremely important that happened on that trip to Jerusalem.

Joseph was still living at the time. We know, therefore, that Joseph died at some point after Jesus was twelve but before he reached age thirty. Jesus was, therefore, highly privileged because in his formative years he had his father and his mother and their love. Both were with him through at least age twelve, and Mary was with him at his death. They taught Jesus wisdom. Moreover, Jesus was by nature gifted. Luke says in fact that "the favor of God was upon him."[7] In other words, the boy seemed to have been both good and destined to be great. And, in the view of his parents and some of his relatives and close friends, he was blessed by God.

We need to establish exactly what occurred at Passover in A.D. 8. It took Mary and Joseph several days to travel from Nazareth to Jerusalem with "their relatives and friends."[8] Among these relatives, presumably, were Jesus' brothers and sisters. He seems to have had four brothers: James, Joseph, Judas, and Simon, and several sisters.[9] We know that, as the Passover festival ended, Mary and Joseph and Jesus' other relatives set off from Jerusalem for the hill country of Judea and/or Nazareth.[10]

Jesus was not, however, in the group. He had been left behind, although his parents did not know it. "Assuming that he was in the group of travelers, they went a day's journey."[11] His parents became concerned at dusk as they "started to look for him among their relatives and friends."[12] When they could not find him, their anxiety grew and became great.[13] They knew immediately what they had to do; that is, to return to Jerusalem to find the boy.

This episode reveals something about Jesus and enables us to say something about his parents. His parents permitted the boy great freedom. They did not over-supervise him, and they trusted him. He was old enough to look after himself, but not of course so old at age twelve to be trusted to be by himself. They did not worry about him because they assumed that he was somewhere in the Nazareth group with his other relatives and friends.

Joseph and Mary returned to Jerusalem. They searched three days for the boy.[14] Finally, they visited the temple and were astounded to find him there. "Child, why have you treated us like this? Look, your father and I have been searching for you in great anxiety."[15] Jesus seems not to have been overly worried about his parents. Nor was he concerned, as an ordinary boy would have been, that his parents, especially at night, would be worried and

13

searching for him. Any other boy would have gone to the temple authorities or even set off after his parents on the road to Nazareth. Jesus' conduct seemed suspect. But his explanation for it makes the seemingly improper conduct highly proper.

Jesus had turned twelve. That is the time in a boy's life when he deems himself to have become a man. Like reaching age eighteen, it is, or it is deemed to be, an official turning point in a boy's life. Jesus thought that he had come of age, although his mother still considered him a child.

Jesus had remained in the temple rather than worry about his parents. He probably figured that his parents would find him there. Given their view of his potential greatness, it is surprising that they did not go immediately to the temple. Jesus' best strategy was, in fact, to wait for his parents in the temple. This is why Jesus answered his mother, "Why were you searching for me? Did you not know that I must be in my Father's house?"[16] Mary and Joseph did not understand, however, what Jesus was saying.[17]

We understand somewhat better. He reasoned that if he were not with his parents, he would be doing the Father's work. He expected his parents to find him in the Father's house. In other words, by age twelve, Jesus had come to know his mission. His answer was not a rejection of Mary and Joseph. It was instead his first affirmation and probably his first recognition, as evident by Mary's surprise, that he was the son of God.[18]

But, while disappointing his parents, Jesus learned something from his three days' stay in the temple and the loving reproach of his mother. He was able to discern the level of his knowledge and knew that he possessed colossal knowledge. After all, when Mary and Joseph went to the temple on the chance that he might be there, "they found him in the temple, sitting among the teachers, listening to them and asking them questions."[19] Jesus could converse with the adults on the Old Testament topics of the day. The teachers found him to be a rather remarkable boy. "[A]ll who heard him were amazed at his understanding and his answers."[20]

14

Something else became apparent, however, as Jesus left the temple with his parents and as they traveled the several days to Nazareth. Jesus came to recognize his limitation. He concluded that he would have to grow up and that he would have to be more patient with his mother and father.[21]

What the episode did was to teach Jesus the value of his father on earth. Hitherto Jesus had taken Joseph for granted. He had heard from the adults, and especially from Zechariah and Elizabeth, and maybe even from their son John, who probably was in the group making the journey toward Nazareth, that he might be the Messiah and was probably the son of God. What Jesus learned from his experience in the temple at age twelve was that he still had more to learn and that he could not do the Father's work until he learned the Father's work.

The years went by, and Jesus was obedient to his parents. He seems to have worked with Joseph in carpentry. The boy "increased in wisdom and in years."[22] His parents and relatives came to view him as a boy blessed both "in divine and human favor."[23]

There is no certainty as to when Joseph died. But the evidence suggests that it might have been far closer to when Jesus reached age thirty than it was to his reaching age twelve. The best hint as to when Joseph died is in Luke. "Then he went down with them and came to Nazareth, and was obedient to them. His mother treasured all these things in her heart. And Jesus increased in wisdom and in years and in divine and human favor."[24] In other words, for the rest of Joseph's life, Jesus was "obedient to them," i.e., to Joseph and Mary. He had lost his impatience. His time would come. But, as Joseph may have taught him, he could not know the day and the hour. Joseph's death was not the occasion for the arrival of that time. Apparently, however, Jesus did not do anything before Joseph's death.

One of the crucial dates in the life of Jesus then is what happened in the "fifteenth year of the reign of Emperor Tiberius."[25] Tiberius reigned from A.D. 14 to A.D. 37, so that this occurred, in other words, in about A.D. 29. During that year, John, on becoming John the Baptist, began his work. And if John the Baptist began his work at about age thirty-three, Jesus could not have begun his work before A.D. 29. This is why Luke argued that "Jesus was *about* thirty years old when he began his work."[26]

The best evidence suggests, however, that Jesus was then thirty-three years old. Clearly, John the Baptist began his work in A.D. 29, and John was six months older than Christ. Thus, we know that Jesus could not have begun his work before A.D. 29.

In that year, John the Baptist was preaching in the wilderness. Jesus was still living in Galilee. "Then Jesus came from Galilee to John at the Jordan, to be baptized by him."[27]

At the Jordan River in about A.D. 29, John hesitated, however, to baptize Jesus. "John would have prevented him [from being baptized]."[28] "I need to be baptized by you, and do you come to me?" asked John.[29]

Jesus was insistent: "Let it be so now; for it is proper for us in this way to fulfill all righteousness."[30] In other words, John thought that by his baptizing Jesus, Jesus would become one of his followers. But John's father had seen the truth: "And you, child, will be called the prophet of the Most High; for you will go before the Lord to prepare his ways."[31]

So the moment came in Jesus' life when, on being baptized by John the Baptist, his childhood and youth were history. Joseph was now long dead. Unmarried, long employed with Joseph as a carpenter, and without children, Jesus set off from his family to commence, as he deemed it, his real work in life. "And when Jesus had been baptized, just as he came up from the water, suddenly the heavens were opened to him and he saw the Spirit of God descending like a dove and alighting on him. And a voice from heaven said, 'This is my Son, the Beloved, with whom I am well pleased.' "[32]

Clearly, therefore, it was Jesus' *baptism* that constituted the *turning point* in his life. All his life had brought him to that moment. His great moment was, of course, his birth. Now, however, the moment came when, as he saw it, he had to effectuate his mission. He had thought that, at age twelve, he could start to do God's work. But that was an illusion and an error he had transcended long ago.

It would, however, be a mistake to believe that, in turning to do his work, Jesus became a disciple of John the Baptist. John the Baptist prepared the way for Jesus Christ. But Jesus Christ was never a disciple of John the Baptist.

Chapter 4
Jesus and John the Baptist

According to Luke, John's birth was no accident. His was a planned birth. Zechariah had prayed for a son.[1] His wife, Elizabeth, was, however, "getting on in years."[2] Zechariah was a rabbi. Both he and Elizabeth strictly followed the commandments and the Mosaic regulations.[3]

Gabriel,[4] an angel of the Most High, appeared to Zechariah in the sanctuary in the hill country of Judea. Gabriel told Zechariah, in a vision, that Elizabeth would bear a son and that the boy should be named John. His mission in life would be to prepare the Jewish people for the coming of the Lord.[5]

John was conceived before Christ and born before him, so that more than theoretically John was the forerunner of Christ.[6] An event of no little significance occurred six months into his life while John was still in his mother's womb. Mary, herself pregnant, came to visit Elizabeth.[7] "When Elizabeth heard Mary's greeting, the child leaped in her womb. And Elizabeth was filled with the Holy Spirit."[8] Elizabeth concluded that Mary necessarily had to be carrying, in the form of a fetus, the one who as an adult would be the "Lord."[9]

As John was born to aging parents, all believed that the hand of the Most High was with him from conception. On the day of his birth in fact, his father proclaimed that John would become the "prophet of the Most High" and "go before the Lord to prepare his

ways, to give knowledge of salvation to his people by the forgiveness of their sins."[10]

About thirty-three years later, in about A.D. 29, and after
preaching briefly in the wilderness, John appeared publicly to Israel
on the Jordan.[11] His message was that the Jews could and would be
saved if they repented. Their repenting was imperative because the
time was near when the Most High would create his kingdom on
earth. "Repent, for the kingdom of heaven has come near."[12]

John's influence spread amongst the Jews. Hundreds of Jews
from the countryside and Jerusalem were attracted to his message.
It seems to have been a time of ferment in Judaism. Many were the
Jews who were baptized by John and who, in the process, confessed
their sins.[13] By turning Jews to baptism, and to salvation through
repenting of their sins, John thought that he was paving the way for
the Messiah.[14]

Unconcerned about his dress, living off of insects and wild
honey,[15] John's preaching, and his activity of baptizing sinners in
the water of the Jordan River, brought him fame throughout Palestine. "Then the people of Jerusalem and all Judea were going out
to him, and all the region along the Jordan, and they were baptized
by him in the river Jordan, confessing their sins."[16]

Whatever was John's message, it seems to have been within
the Jewish tradition. John was winning these Jews to baptism
because his message was appealing, it served a need, and it was not
antagonistic to Judaism. John's stress on the revengefulness of God
and of God's "wrath to come" was emphatically Jewish.[17] In John's
view, and in his view of God, God tired of impenitence. "Even now
the ax is lying at the root of the trees; every tree therefore that does
not bear good fruit is cut down and thrown into the fire."[18]

Jews necessarily, therefore, had to repent. "I baptize you with
water for repentance."[19] However, in John's view, baptism alone
would not mean salvation. Salvation would come via the Messiah.
"[O]ne who is more powerful than I is coming; I am not worthy to

19

untie the thong of his sandals. He will baptize you with the Holy Spirit and fire."[20]

Thus, according to John, baptism by water would, so to say, wash away the sinner's sins. But the sinner had to undergo yet another baptism: this would be by the Holy Spirit. Only when their lives had been changed by the Holy Spirit would committing sins be passé in their history. Clearly, then, John gave "knowledge of salvation to [the Jewish] people by the forgiveness of their sins."[21]

John believed that the God of Israel would redeem the Jews. Redemption would come through, however, the arrival of a Messiah. John's perspective was messianic Judaism. God would bring a new day to the Jews. Their sins would be forgiven. The light on that new day would show the way to salvation. The Messiah would extirpate their sins.[22]

It should be noted, however, that John did not view himself as the Messiah. He believed himself the messenger, the one who had been sent ahead to announce the coming of the Messiah.[23] Necessarily, in John's view, the Messiah would be the "Son of God."[24] Thus, because of the impending arrival of the Messiah, the Jews would have to repent because the kingdom of heaven was at hand.

While there is no direct information about John's ethno-religious background, circumstantial evidence compels the conclusion that John's parents were messianic Jews and probably Essenes. His origin as an Essene or at least within messianic Judaism can be derived from the perspective of his parents. Although Zechariah, his father, was said to be righteous and a firm adherent to the commandments and the Mosaic regulations, his fundamentalism would not necessarily exclude messianic Judaism. Indeed, it would seem to be part and parcel of it.

In Zechariah's perspective, as in John's, and later Christ's, the Jewish ecclesiastical establishment in Jerusalem did not play a central role in the redemption of the Jews. Although said to be from Gabriel, Zechariah accepted the view of a Messiah and of John the Baptist's role in turning " 'many of the people of Israel to the Lord their God' " by making the Jews " 'prepared for the [coming of the] Lord.' "[25]

What had happened in the scores of years before 6 B.C. was that messianic Judaism found a wide adherence amongst the Jews. If then, as is our thesis, Zechariah and Elizabeth were messianic Jews, perhaps even Essenic Jews, the conclusion would seem to be warranted that their relatives, Mary and Jesus, and perhaps even Joseph, at least to an extent, were Essenes. Zechariah certainly believed, in any event, that his son, John, would become a prophet of the Lord, with the task of giving knowledge to the Jews of the way to salvation. John remained within Judaism, although, of course, he was outside of its mainstream.

The conclusion is compelled then that John the Baptist constituted the last of the great Jewish prophets.[26] John the Baptist's movement was not part of the Christian movement. While several of John the Baptist's followers might have become Christians, Christianity developed separately from, although it arose almost simultaneously with, the John the Baptist movement.

Jesus' view of John is significant. He considered John to be the forerunner, the messenger, the one who prepared the way for the new covenant, or, that is, Christianity. "This [i.e., John] is the one about whom it is written, 'See, I am sending my messenger ahead of you, who will prepare your way before you.' "[27]

John the Baptist brought Judaism to a new stage in its development. As practiced by many sects, but most prominently by the John the Baptist movement, messianic Judaism held that the God of Israel would redeem the Jews by sending a savior or, that is, a Messiah. Christianity took from John the Baptist and his movement their core message of salvation by baptism and a Messiah through the coming of the Kingdom of God.

John did not know the Messiah. He deemed, however, Jesus to be the "Lamb of God who takes away the sin of the world."[28] His parents,[29] the baptism of Jesus,[30] and the message that John received in prison from Jesus[31] increasingly impressed that view upon him.

21

Chapter 5

Becoming Jesus Christ

In about A.D. 29, Jesus came from Nazareth to John at the Jordan River in Judea "to be baptized by him."[1] John hesitated to baptize Jesus. As he did so, however, something extraordinary occurred.

The baptism confirmed, and it revealed, Jesus' mission. In fact, it was the exact point where the spirit of God was finally, after all the speculation, revealed to Jesus. Jesus learned at that moment that, as he believed, he was actually the son of God. He became at his baptism, moreover, what he had been developing into, namely, Jesus Christ.

As he was being baptized or was coming out of the water and was praying to the Most High, Jesus had a vision. In the vision, the heavens were opened and the Holy Spirit seemed to descend upon him in the form of a dove. Jesus heard a voice from heaven saying, " 'You are my beloved Son; with you I am well pleased.' "[2] John also saw the dove. Thus, at the moment of Jesus' baptism, because of the visions, both Jesus and John the Baptist were confirmed in their view that Jesus was the son of God.[3]

Jesus was then "about thirty years old,"[4] that is to say, he was in fact thirty-three. His baptism constituted the very moment when Jesus began his work. We are dating the origin of Christianity, therefore, from about the spring of A.D. 29. Its birthplace was there in, or on the bank of, the Jordan River.

After being baptized, Jesus left the Jordan. "[F]ull of the Holy Spirit," he went into the wilderness.[5] He fasted there forty days. Famished, and without much strength, Christ seemed to see the

22

devil. Christ understood that it was Satan's purpose to confuse him and to get him to believe he was not really the son of God. The devil was, in fact, Machiavellian. Satan would have Christ disbelieve the vision at his baptism.

Jesus had not spent, however, thirty-three years with the carpenter and in discussions with the rabbis about the Old Testament for nothing. More than a generation had passed since he had the intuition and the first insight into the fact that he happened to be, or he sensed that others would believe him to be, the son of God. He had "increased in wisdom and in years, and in divine and human favor."[6] He was now to do battle with the evil spirit on behalf of the Holy Spirit.

Satan knew that Christ was famished and in a weak condition. But, from the perspective of the devil, that was the perfect condition. Jesus recalled Satan's first temptation: "If you are the Son of God, command this stone to become a loaf of bread."[7] Jesus answered that, in its time, bread, of course, was a wonderful thing. It was a human necessity. But it was not alone the only thing in life. "It is written," said Jesus, " 'One does not live by bread alone, but by every word that comes from the mouth of God.' "[8] Thus, Christ learned here that Satan could not tempt him with *material* things. Material things, such as gold or money, are necessary in many cases. But, vis-à-vis doing God's work, for Jesus, they were not important, and certainly not the main thing.

Perhaps, however, although not influenced by material things, Satan could tempt Jesus by turning him against the Holy Spirit. Satan tried, therefore, to cause Jesus, in his condition, to repudiate his vision and to deny that he was the son of God by another temptation: that, if he jumped from the roof of the temple in Jerusalem, he would still live because God would intervene to save him.[9] Jesus refused to attempt suicide, thereby putting God to the test of saving him, to prove that God happened to be God and he himself the son of God. "It is said," Jesus explained, " 'Do not put the Lord your God to the test.' "[10]

23

But, born amongst humans, perhaps Christ had an ego so that he was fascinated by power and fame. The evil spirit showed Christ, in a vision, all the kingdoms of the world.[11] Christ recalled Satan's tempting him by saying, " 'To you I will give their glory and all this authority; for it has been given over to me, and I [can] give it to anyone I please.' "[12] "All these I will give you, if you will fall down and worship me."[13] Jesus, however, rejected world power and glory. "Away with you, Satan! for it is written, 'Worship the Lord your God, and serve only him.' "[14]

Forty days in the wilderness and the struggle against the devil had taught Christ that, although human, he did not seek earthly power, fame, or fortune. However, the experience had confirmed to him the need to be careful because foolish acts might put the Lord his God to the test of having to intervene to save him.

And so, in A.D. 29, Jesus left the wilderness. John was then in Bethany across from the Jordan River.[15] Some priests and Levites had been sent from the Jerusalem ecclesiastical establishment to investigate John. On behalf of the Pharisees, they wanted to know why he was baptizing if he were "neither the Messiah, nor Elijah, nor the prophet?"[16] John told them that he baptized only with water. Another, coming after him, had the mission of baptizing with the Holy Spirit.[17]

On the following day, John saw Jesus approaching and openly proclaimed, "Here is the Lamb of God who takes away the sin of the world! This is he of whom I said, 'After me comes a man who ranks ahead of me because he was before me.' I myself did not know him; but I came baptizing with water for this reason, that he might be revealed to Israel."[18]

John the Baptist revealed to his disciples, therefore, that Jesus was the Messiah and "the Son of God."[19] John's pronouncement electrified some of his disciples. Thus, just as Jesus prepared to go his own way, John the Baptist prepared the way amongst his own followers for their acceptance of Jesus as the son of God.

Two of John's disciples left him to follow Jesus when John

said this again on the following day.[20] One of these disciples was Andrew. Andrew went and got Peter, his brother, saying that John the Baptist had revealed to them that Jesus happened to be the Messiah or, that is, the one *anointed* by God.[21] Two other of Jesus' future disciples, James and John, were fishing with their father Zebedee and his employees in a boat when Jesus, now Jesus Christ, called out to them that they should follow him.[22]

Clearly, as he gathered about him his twelve disciples and his host of followers, including an exceptionally large number of women, Christ felt his power. He seems to have had colossal charisma and an extremely forceful and attractive character aided by a powerful insight into the nature of the human mind, into God's will, and into the unfolding of human history. In addition, of course, he could cast out demons from the afflicted. And, when necessary, he could perform certain so-called miracles.

Among the things that Jesus could do, especially to exhibit signs of his glory sufficiently to confirm his power to his disciples and their belief in him as the Messiah and/or the son of God, was to cause a mass of people at a party to believe that water had become wine. And, in fact, as they tasted it, whether it was water or wine, they believed it to be wine so that, for them, it was wine. "Jesus did this, [performing] the first of his signs, in Cana of Galilee, and revealed [thereby] his glory; and his disciples believed in him."[23] "And he cured many who were sick with various diseases, and cast out many demons."[24]

Jesus had come by then to treasure his relationship with his father, Joseph. As we have intimated, at age twelve, Jesus took this relationship for granted. But, in the later years, he saw that, in selecting Joseph to shepherd him through birth and to maturity, God had picked an excellent man. Moreover, Jesus knew something else: he might be the son of God, but on earth he was the son of Joseph, that is, the son of man. While not denying that he was the "Son of God" and the "King of Israel,"[25] Jesus stressed the fact that because Joseph had adopted and reared him, he was Joseph's son, the son of man.[26]

Owing to the miracles, the curing of the sick, the casting out of demons from the afflicted, and his teaching in the synagogues of Galilee, Jesus' fame spread throughout Galilee, Jordan, Syria, and all Palestine.[27] His message was, in brief, the "good news" of the coming of God's kingdom on earth. He "proclaim[ed] the message" throughout Galilee.[28] His greatest defeat before April 5, A.D. 30, was also, however, in Galilee and, paradoxically, in Nazareth.

As was his custom while living in Nazareth, he went to the synagogue on Saturday. On this particular visit, Jesus stood up to read. Someone gave him a scroll on which was written the Book of Isaiah. Jesus unrolled the scroll and found the passages he wanted to read in Hebrew:

> The spirit of the Lord is upon me, because he has *anointed* me to bring good news to the poor. He has sent me to proclaim release to the captives and recovery of sight to the blind, to let the oppressed go free, to proclaim the year of the Lord's favor.[29]

At that point, after reading the passage and returning the Dead Sea-type scroll to the attendant, Jesus astonished the synagogue by saying, "Today this scripture has been fulfilled in your hearing."[30]

Since he suggested their incorrigibility and averred that he happened to be the one anointed, the Messiah, the whole synagogue, including some of his relatives, were enraged. The hometown folks drove him from Nazareth, and if he had not escaped, they would have murdered him by pushing him off the Nazareth cliff.[31]

Driven out of Nazareth, and with John the Baptist in a Roman prison,[32] Jesus began to proclaim the need for repentance. "The time is fulfilled, and the kingdom of God has come near; repent, and believe in the good news."[33]

Chapter 6
Jesus' View of God

We know that Jesus could trace his lineage from David and alleged-ly even from Adam, the so-called first man.[1] A second well-known fact is that Jesus' biological mother, Mary, was Jewish. We have circumstantial evidence suggesting in fact that Jesus was an Essene. It is clear, in any case, that Jesus was reared in the Jewish religious tradition.

How then did Jesus, a Jew, become Christian? What exactly was the Jewish view of God? What was Jesus' mature view of God? And regardless of the development of Jesus' view of God, what, because of Jesus, is the **Christian** view of God?

The Jewish view of God developed deep in Jewish history. The Jews themselves trace it back at least to Abraham. Abraham was born in the land of the Chaldeans.[2] There is strong evidence that the Chaldeans demanded, or at least they wanted, the Jews to follow the Chaldean gods. But apparently the Jews preferred to worship another God, "the God they had come to know."[3] Their ancestors in Chaldea "drove them out from the presence of their gods."[4] The Jews fled to Mesopotamia. It was there in the city of Ur, in today's Iraq, that Abraham was born.[5]

Out of the land of the Chaldeans, the Jews brought with them their traditions and those traditions acceptable to them acquired from and during their stay in Mesopotamia. The Jews, through Abraham's family, had their own conception of religion and, there-fore, of God.

27

There was something about Abraham's character that compelled him to be amenable to foreign adventure.[6] Abraham's conception of God reveals, at the same time, Abraham's character. As we come to understand Abraham's character and his psychology, we will come to know the Jewish view of God.

Abraham died when he was, in early Jewish years, 175 years old.[7] It is not Abraham's death but his age at his departure from Mesopotamia that is of concern to us. Abraham seems to have been a relatively young man at age seventy-five. More than a third of his life had passed. He then had no offspring because, as was thought, his wife, Sarai, was barren.[8] In a vision, or a dream, Abraham came to understand that he should continue his father's journey from Mesopotamia.[9]

It is clear that Abraham left Mesopotamia because he had been drawn by the attractive socio-economic situation obtaining in Palestine.[10] Palestine then was controlled by the Canaanites or, in effect, the Palestinians.[11] Abraham concluded, however, that, in a vision, his God had told him: "To your offspring I will give this land."[12] The Jews lived in Palestine until the famine. "There they settled, and grew very prosperous in gold and silver and very much livestock."[13] There came about, therefore, the confluence of a land that enabled the Jews to grow prosperous with, as Abraham viewed it, the will of their God.[14]

Abraham wanted Palestine for his progeny. The mass of land he desired seemed to have been, however, more than Palestine or Palestine was deemed to be, or Israel would be, all the land between the Mesopotamian frontier and the Egyptian border. If Palestine were not all of that area, the Jews subsequently envisioned Palestine as something of a Greater Israel. Israel would be the area from the Sinai to and through Lebanon, Palestine, significant portions of Jordan, much of Syria, and that portion of Iraq up to the Euphrates River.[15]

The Jews did not own the land. Other peoples were in those lands and owned them. The Jews planned, however, to dispossess these people and to take their land. And, in the view of the Jews, their God entered into a covenant with them and had no concern for the peoples of those lands. Their God, after all, was *their* God and not the God of the people in Palestine.

It should not be so surprising, therefore, that to the Jews, God appeared to be a *Jewish* God. Their God, Yahweh, became in the main a tribal deity leading the Jewish tribe in battle against the other nations for the creation of a Greater Israel. Yahweh became a particularized God, a God serving the Jewish people, a Jewish God. Moreover, for the Jews, Yahweh was not a universal God, but their own, and their exclusive, God.

As Abraham recalled, the Jewish God first appeared in Abraham's mind in a dream or a vision and proposing a *quid pro quo*. The Jewish God announced that, in Hebrew, he was *El Shaddai* or, as translated, God Almighty. *El Shaddai* proposed to become exclusively the God of Abraham and his offspring if Abraham would "walk before [*El Shaddai*], and be blameless."[16] Thus, under the covenant, Abraham and his offspring were to be irreproachable in conduct and thought and serve *El Shaddai*. In return, since the covenant was "everlasting" in that it would last as long as there were Abraham's offspring, *El Shaddai* would give the Jews "all the land of Canaan, for a perpetual holding."[17] At the same time, *El Shaddai* would become "their God."[18] In other words, *El Shaddai* would "be God to [Abraham] and to [Abraham's] offspring."[19]

Clearly, then, *El Shaddai*, as God Almighty, would be a God limited to Abraham and his progeny, that is, to Jews. But, as part and parcel and a sign of the covenant, Abraham, his male offspring, and any male foreigner under Jewish rule, would have to be circumcised so that, by use of a blade or a knife against the "flesh of [the] foreskin" on their penises, the covenant would be, so to say, "in [the male] flesh."[20]

While the Jews were in Egypt, one of Abraham's offspring, Moses, urged the Jews to be nationalistic.[21] Jewish tradition has it that Moses was able to communicate with *El Shaddai*. *El Shaddai* appeared to Moses out of the flame of a bush that would not burn. *El Shaddai* announced that he had observed the misery of "my people [the Jews] who are in Egypt."[22] The Jewish God promised to bring the Jews from Egypt into "the country of the Canaanites, the Hittites, the Amorites, the Perizzites, the Hivites, and Jebusites."[23] The Jews would rule Palestine and/or create a Greater Israel, extending from "the Red Sea to the Sea of the Philistines, and from the wilderness to the Euphrates."[24]

Thus, the Jewish God reaffirmed the covenant with the Jews. Moses, however, wanted to know the name of the Jewish God. What, besides *El Shaddai*, or God Almighty, were the Jews to call their God? *El Shaddai* answered, "I Am Who I Am."[25] Thus, the Jewish God would be called by his name and his title: "YHWH [pronounced Yahweh], the God of your ancestors, the God of Abraham, the God of Isaac, and the God of Jacob."[26] The Jewish God was to be called *Yahweh, the Jewish God* or "[Yahweh], the God of the Hebrews."[27] Jews could not invoke the name of other gods.[28] They would know their God by his name, Yahweh, and by his title, that is, the God of Israel. "I am YHWH [Yahweh]. I appeared to Abraham, Isaac, and Jacob as *El Shaddai*, but by my name '[YHWH]' I did not make myself known to them."[29]

The Jews had and have, therefore, their conception of God. Moses and Aaron, two of the early and greatest of the Jewish leaders, for example, went to the African king, the Pharaoh of Egypt, and said, in their argument for letting the Jews go from Egypt and its slavery: "Thus said [Yahweh], the God of Israel, 'Let my people go, so that they may celebrate a festival to me in the wilderness.' "[30] The Egyptian Pharaoh noted that he did not know Yahweh. Moses and Aaron explained that Yahweh was their God, the "God of the Hebrews."[31]

We know, therefore, that, in the Jewish view, their God was Yahweh, the God of Israel. We must now establish, however, Yahweh's nature as revealed to the Jews through the visions and/or dreams of Abraham, Moses, and certain other of their prophets and/or leaders.

According to the Jews, their God was omnipotent. Their God could, for example, create the Solar System and the earth presumably by commanding it.[32] While God Almighty could call such things into being, their God could also act on matter, that is, for example, separate "the light from the darkness."[33] Thus, God Almighty created the heavens and the earth, but, as viewed by the Hebrews, God Almighty did it in six days. More importantly, according to Jewish tradition, God Almighty created Adam and Eve, or male and female human beings, "in his image, in the image of God he created them; male and female he created them."[34] Presumably, therefore, with the assistance of angels, God Almighty made the earth while the angels and God Almighty served as the model for the construction of humankind. "When God created humankind, he made them in the likeness of God."[35]

The Jews had a peculiar view of the relationship between their God, humanity, and the earth. In their view, humans would subdue, that is, overpower by superior force or "have dominion over," the flora and fauna of earth.[36] Their God created the first humans, Adam and Eve, and put them in a garden, known as Eden, located somewhere "in the east," that is, in the east from Israel.[37] The implication is that Eden, the place where the flora and fauna were cultivated, was somewhere over near today's Iraq. This conclusion is an obvious one because there was a river that flowed through the garden. At some point, downstream, the river separated into "four branches."[38] Two of these branches, the Tigris River and the Euphrates River,[39] are found in Iraq.

Ostensibly, had Adam and Eve not eaten food from the "tree of the knowledge of good and evil," humans would have had everlasting life on earth.[40] In other words, God Almighty entered into a covenant with Adam, and through Adam with Eve. But, influenced by Eve, Adam broke the covenant and God Almighty became vengeful. The serpent was made to crawl in the dust through eternity.[41] Women, or Eve, were to have children in pain and come under the hegemony of men,[42] while men, or Adam, were to toil the soil in order to obtain food and be returned to the ground at death.[43]

The Jews took over or arrived at a conception of God as the Almighty God. This God had a covenant between himself and humanity. In the Jewish view, however, after Adam and Eve broke the covenant and because the then-existing humankind were said to be inclined toward evil and their wickedness knew no limitation,[44] Almighty God extirpated all the peoples of the earth except Noah, his wife, and their sons and his daughter-in-laws, the ancestors of the Semite peoples.[45]

Thus, in the Jewish view, God Almighty then entered into another, or a *third*, covenant and thereby changed his nature. God Almighty became or was revealed to be Yahweh, their God, the God of Israel. Yahweh was not the Semite God, because the Semites worshiped other gods. Nor was Yahweh the God of those peoples outside of the Middle East. Rather, Yahweh was exclusively a Jewish God. And, moreover, this God, the Jewish God, was a vengeful, harsh, and jealous God. As Moses says Yahweh told him, " 'You shall tear down their [the non-Jewish Greater Israel peoples'] altars, break their pillars, and cut down their sacred poles (for you shall worship no other god, because [Yahweh], whose name is Jealous, is a jealous God).' "[46]

It is important to note that from God Almighty with (1) a covenant with humanity and then God Almighty with (2) a covenant with Noah and his extended family or the Semite peoples generally, God Almighty became or was turned into (3) a wrathful God, the God of Abraham. Under the second covenant, the one with Noah and his Semite tribal family, the human family from which came the Jews, the Semites "could not eat flesh with its life, that is, its blood."[47] God Almighty pledged, however, that "never again shall all flesh be cut off by the waters of a flood, and never again shall there be a flood to destroy the earth."[48] From a universal God, God Almighty became, eventually, according to the Jews, a Jewish God.

Jewish tradition has it in fact that the third covenant arose because their Semite ancestors, including the Chaldeans, came to worship other gods. The Jews had "abandoned" the worship of these other gods and had come to a monotheistic religious view so that they worshiped "the God of heaven, the God they had come to know."[49]

Through their leaders, from Abraham to Moses and on through their prophets, the Jews converted "the God of heaven" into a *Jewish* God. Moses claimed, however, that their view dovetailed with that of God Almighty. "[Y]ou are a people holy to [Yahweh] your God; it is you [Yahweh] has chosen out of all the peoples on earth to be his people, his treasured possession."[50] Under this view, since God Almighty was or became exclusively the God of Israel, the Jews could "utterly [destroy the non-Jewish] men, women, and children" in taking their land and their possessions.[51]

The evidence is compelling, then, that Yahweh was exclusively "their God," i.e., the God of Israel.[52] "I am [Yahweh] your God, who brought you out of the land of Egypt, out of the house of slavery; you shall have no other gods before me."[53]

The covenant between Yahweh and the Jews was not a covenant between God and humanity. Far from a God for all humanity, Yahweh was, or this God became, a Jewish tribal God. "I am [Yahweh] your God."[54] "I will establish my covenant between me and you, and your offspring after you throughout their generations, for an everlasting covenant, to be God to you and to your offspring after you."[55]

The third covenant was to be solely between Yahweh and Abraham and his progeny, the Jews. Their God, Yahweh, "set his heart in love on your ancestors alone and chose" the Jews "out of all the peoples."[56] "I will take you as my people, and I will be your God."[57] "I will dwell among the Israelites, and I will be their God. And they shall know I am [Yahweh] their God, who brought them out of the land of Egypt that I might dwell among them; I am [Yahweh] their God."[58] Yahweh, therefore, was the Jewish God. As Moses put it, "Hear, O Israel: [Yahweh] is our God, [Yahweh] alone."[59] "I who brought you out of the land of Egypt to be your God: I am [Yahweh]."[60]

Significantly, the Jews believed that only they had a God. "[F]or there is no one like you, and there is no God besides you."[61] "And you established your people Israel for yourself to be your people forever; and you, O [Yahweh], became their God."[62] "For who is God, but [Yahweh]?"[63]

We have established that Jesus was born Jewish. He was even circumcised pursuant to the Jewish tradition. Unless other evidence compels a different conclusion, it would follow that Jesus held the Jewish view of God as we have delineated it. In the Jewish view, Yahweh served as their God, but Yahweh never became a universal God, a God for all humanity.

What then was Christ's view of God? Did Jesus worship Yahweh and, if so, at what point, if at any point, did he achieve self-clarification? There must have been a reason, in other words, why Jesus, the Son of God, spent "about thirty years"[64] being educated at home and in the synagogue. Luke tells us frankly that "Jesus increased in wisdom and in years, and in divine and human favor."[65] As part of this increase in wisdom, Jesus learned more about God and God's nature. Luke clearly implies that, although gifted, Jesus did not start out at birth with knowledge of God. The implication is that he came to this knowledge.

There seems to be no reason to question that the Jewish view of God was Jesus' view of God through about age twelve. It is no secret, however, that, because of Jesus and his movement, the Bible came to include a segment called the "New Testament." In other words, as he increased in wisdom, Christ came to, and revealed, a new convenant. At least, if Christianity exists as a religion, it must have been Jesus who articulated the doctrine. Members of his party, and especially the gospel writers, only elucidated it. Jesus' development, including his becoming aware of the nature of God, constituted a lifelong process.

Jesus' perspective from age twelve to about age thirty, and his point of view even after he commenced his work, still remained Jewish. He still believed that he had been sent by Yahweh.

Proof of this is not difficult. Jesus sent his twelve disciples, all Jews, out to preach. "Go nowhere among the Gentiles, and enter no town of the Samaritans, but go rather to the lost sheep of the house of Israel. As you go, proclaim the good news, 'The kingdom of heaven has come near.' "[66] But what happened as he went into "the district of Tyre and Sidon,"[67] that is, into Lebanon, revealed that Jesus was still limited by his Jewish background.

A Palestinian woman in Lebanon shouted at him, "Have mercy on me, Lord, Son of David; my daughter is tormented by a demon."[68] Matthew tells us that although his disciples urged him to render aid to the woman's daughter in her fight against Satan, Jesus, who specialized in fighting demons in the human mind, would not answer her.

Jesus' reply revealed his limitation and his perspective: "I was sent only to the lost sheep of the house of Israel."[69] As a human being, Christ was a Jew. He thought the Palestinians inferior. He had come to believe that he was sent, and sent by Yahweh, to save the Jews.

The Gospel sources do not tell us much about this "Canaanite woman from that [Tyre and Sidon] region."[70] But it is clear that she played a significant role in the formation of the Christian doctrine. It was she who forced Christ, and forced him by her faith, to tend those sheep outside the flock of Israel. She compelled him to broaden his doctrine from a Jewish to a world doctrine.

Matthew explains that, at that moment, Jesus grew in stature, matured in wisdom, and became other than himself. A revolution had occurred practically, if not yet theoretically, in his thinking. "Then Jesus answered her, 'Woman, great is your faith! Let it be done for you as you wish.' And her daughter was healed instantly."[71]

Matthew does not mention it overtly, but the significance of the rendezvous with the Syro-Phoenician woman was not lost on Jesus and should not escape us. A new era had opened in the history of the Christian party. Christianity had breached its Jewish point of origin and had made the turn toward becoming a world religion. Although only in embryo, it had become a doctrine applicable, like democracy, to all peoples.

We usually think that the break between Judaism and Christianity or, in short, the origin of Christianity lies with Jesus. The evidence, however, is compelling: Jesus was Christian, but, until his meeting the Syro-Phoenician woman, he thought his aim was to save only the Jews.

Jesus had told his followers in fact to beware of "the teaching of the Pharisees and Sadducees."[72] In other words, Jesus was still trying to substitute his doctrine of Christianity into the shell of Judaism. In reality, however, Christianity is the opposite of Judaism. It arose out of, but it constitutes a break with, Judaism. It cannot be described as a new form of Judaism or a return to its essence. Jesus did not really understand this fact, however, even after meeting the Syro-Phoenician woman.

What Jesus did not do, but what, based on this episode, he should have done was to have turned radically toward building a base in the Palestinian and/or Gentile community. The Christian party eventually would learn the lesson and find their greatest success outside Israel. John, therefore, has Christ saying before his death in Jerusalem so as to imply that Christ then, perhaps from this episode with the Syro-Phoenician woman, had come over to another view of God: "I have other sheep [Gentiles] that do not belong to this fold [Israel]. I must bring them also, and they will listen to my voice. So there will be one flock, one shepherd."[73] It is the probable position of Christ. But, while in Christ's words, it was the lesson learned or fully learned by Christ and his disciples from their whole experience in Galilee and in Jerusalem and through the crucifixion.

We can conclude, then, that Jesus thought himself to be both a Jew and a proponent of Judaism. The wise men had worshiped him, after all, as the " 'king of the Jews.' "[74] They may have helped Christ to see his mission. But, at the same time, they might have contributed to his failure to see his true nature until it was, for him, too late. Thus, Jesus believed himself to be, among other things, a Jewish prophet. He conceived of his mission as that of purifying Judaism.

Jesus was, in truth, another Jewish prophet. The Jewish masses were not incorrect. But neither were the members of the Jewish ecclesiastical establishment. Where the Jewish masses saw Jesus as a prophet,[75] the Jewish ecclesiastical establishment viewed him, his party, and his doctrine, as outside Judaism. And, in fact, he was substituting another doctrine for Judaism.

Where then did Jesus achieve his self-education so that he came to another view of God? There certainly must be a point where Christianity separated from Judaism and therefore the Christian view of a universal God for all the people departed from the Jewish view of Yahweh as the Jewish people's exclusive God.

John implies that the new outlook came to Jesus at a moment shortly before his arrest.[76] "The law indeed was given through Moses; grace and truth [i.e., the truth about God] came through Jesus Christ. No one has ever seen God. It is God the only Son, who is close to the Father's heart, who has made him known."[77]

Although John might be right, it was, in our view, the trial, execution, and the "resurrection" of Jesus that revealed this truth to Jesus' disciples.[78] Thus, at some point between the crucifixion and the resurrection of Christ, Jesus' disciples became Christians. At that moment, their conception of God was transformed into the perspective of God as a universal God. From Yahweh and a covenant with the Jews, there arose a new and/or fourth covenant that involved God Almighty and all humanity as revealed through Jesus Christ.

In this new view, God was not just one entity. Nor was God

Yahweh, the Jewish God. As a unity, however, there was one God. God was the Father, the Son, and the Holy Spirit.[79] And, instead of Yahweh, the God of Israel, God Almighty had been revealed to be the God "[i]n the beginning," that is, the God of "the heavens and the earth."[80]

What Jesus did, therefore, was to create a new covenant. Basically, the new covenant constituted a return, at a higher stage of development, to the first covenant. As John noted, none of the prophets and/or Semite or Jewish leaders, whether Noah, Abraham or Moses, knew God. Moses received the law from God. But the "truth" about God's nature "came through [i.e., from] Jesus Christ."[81]

At his death then, Jesus transcended his Jewish background and his Jewish view of God and, according to his disciples, he was resurrected into heaven. In the process, Jesus transcended the view of God Almighty as *Lord and Governor* with a covenant exclusively with the Jews and brought his disciples to the view of God Almighty as the *Father* with a covenant embracing all humanity.[82]

Chapter 7

Jesus and the Kingdom of God on Earth

As a minister of the gospel and a teacher with enormous analytical and expository power, Jesus traveled throughout Galilee.[1] He went "through the cities and villages proclaiming and bringing the good news of the kingdom of God."[2] Great crowds "followed him from Galilee, the Decapolis, Jerusalem, Judea, and from beyond the Jordan."[3]

Jesus taught the multitude. His object, however, was to carry the "good news of God" to the poor.[4] Jesus urged both the poor and the multitude to change their ways. They were encouraged to repent, to be baptized, and to believe in the "message."[5]

Since, from the time of John the Baptist's arrest, Jesus spent his mature days "proclaiming the message" to the multitude,[6] it is necessary, somewhat in detail, to outline the exact nature of this message. If Christianity is anything, its *message*, including its view of God, surely gives to it its widespread appeal.

Jesus' message was essentially that the multitude should "Repent, for the kingdom of heaven has come near."[7] He taught in other words, that: "The time is fulfilled, and the kingdom of God has come near; repent, and believe in the good news."[8]

The message, therefore, was that of the coming of the Kingdom of God. In Jesus' view, God would establish his kingdom on earth. In fact, the kingdom was already being established.

Those who were poor, and especially poor in spirit, were prime

39

candidates for the kingdom of heaven.[9] As Jesus put it, "Blessed are those who hunger and thirst for righteousness, for they will be filled."[10]

According to Jesus, a new type of revolution, a revolution transforming the mind, or the human spirit, would occur on earth. The arrogant would be displaced by the meek. Those poor in spirit would be enriched by the Holy Spirit. Both the meek and the poor would enter the Kingdom of God. Those who had given up evil and become "pure in heart" would constitute eventually the kingdom's population.[11] And God's kingdom would be established on earth.[12]

In the Kingdom of God, peace would reign, because evil would be banished from the human mind and there would be no need for war.[13] Once, in their hearts and minds, the people came to the Ten Commandments, the Kingdom of God would come into being.[14] As adhered to by the people, the Ten Commandments served as the precursor of, and constituted the gateway into, the Kingdom of God.

The formation of the Kingdom of God fulfilled God's will on earth just "as it is in heaven."[15] At the gate to or on entering into the Kingdom of God, humans would be rescued from evil.[16] Humans would not know evil because they would have come to be good and, therefore, to know God.

It must be made clear, however, that Jesus had no plan to save the righteous. They were, after all, already saved. Jesus wanted, therefore, to save the sinners because, in his view, the unrighteous could become righteous.[17]

Jesus believed that the kingdom of heaven had not been finally established. It had only " 'come near.' "[18] The kingdom was so near, in fact, that its formation was just around the corner. "Truly I tell you," said Jesus, "there are some standing here who will not taste death before they see the Son of Man coming in his kingdom."[19]

Apparently, one entered the kingdom of heaven. From there, one then proceeded to heaven. Thus, in Jesus' view, God's reign is established on earth. But this reign, ironically, would be in the hearts and minds of men and women. Thus, in the Kingdom of God, there would be a gathering of the righteous. Both those into evil and those inclined toward good would travel the same road until the morning of the formation of the Kingdom of God on earth.[20] From one country, and spreading to all countries, the Kingdom of God would become a whole and come to be one gigantic entity.[21]

The conclusion is compelled then that both those who are good and those who are into evil can get into the kingdom. Nevertheless, the Kingdom of God would be a kingdom of those who were righteous. This is because, once in the kingdom, the power of God would separate those who were good from those who were evil. "The Son of Man will send his angels, and they will collect out of his kingdom all causes of sin and all evildoers, and they will throw them into the furnace of fire, where there will be weeping and gnashing of teeth. Then the righteous will shine like the sun in the kingdom of their Father."[22] The formation of the Kingdom of God would be "like a net that was thrown into the sea and caught fish of every kind; when it was full, they drew it ashore, sat down, and put the good into baskets but threw out the bad."[23]

One could save oneself by good work and enter the Kingdom of God, but good work alone would not get one into heaven.[24] Both those who are good and those into evil may enter into, and are even invited to, the Kingdom of God. But, once there, only the few are chosen to go into heaven.[25] God selected, and God preordained, those who would enter heaven. "[T]o sit at my right hand and at my left, this is not mine to grant, but it is for those for whom it has been prepared by my Father."[26]

As Jesus developed and grew wiser, however, he modified his view about the arrival of the Kingdom of God. He came to the conclusion that human society was pregnant with the Kingdom of God. But its birth was at some point in the future.

Jesus seems to have concluded that the whole world would have to come simultaneously to the stage where the gate opened to the kingdom.[27] Thus, before the Kingdom of God arrived, humans would experience many things, from famines to earthquakes and wars and rumors of wars to a host of false prophets attempting to lead the multitude astray.[28]

As it turned out, however, Jesus himself did not know the day and the hour or the season and the year of the formation of the Kingdom of God. "[A]bout that day and hour no one knows, neither the angels of heaven, nor the Son, but only the Father."[29] Jesus concluded that the Kingdom of God would come "at an unexpected hour."[30] It is being born. But the day of its birth could not be predicted. "Keep awake therefore, for you know neither the day nor the hour."[31]

Increasingly, it seems, Jesus conflated the time that people would spend in the Kingdom of God into the moment the elected would enter heaven. Humans would be taken into heaven after or as the good were separated from the bad and as the bad are thrown "into eternal punishment."[32] At that moment, Satan's power would be cut short and Satan's rule would be liquidated.

Jesus seems to have concluded that the Kingdom of God was already in existence, but not finally formed. In fact, he argued, the "kingdom of God is among [i.e., within] you."[33] The important thing for those afflicted with evil, then, was to repent. Repentance meant, and it was in essence, forsaking evil and coming to love oneself, others, nature, and God.

Chapter 8

The Role of Love in Jesus' Perspective

Increasingly human psychology is being revealed to be formed on the basis of parental love for the child and the child's love for his and/or her parents.[1] Love is to Christianity as the Nile is to Egypt. In fact, the secret of Christianity has to be sought in love.

While Moses revealed, as they are called, the Ten Commandments,[2] and while the Jews were to love their God,[3] the Jews had to love their God because they *feared* Yahweh.[4] "[Yahweh] your God you shall fear."[5] "Do what is right and good in the sight of [Yahweh], so that it may go well with you."[6]

Jesus thought, however, that while the commandments were good, and should be adhered to, the focus ought to be on love. "They who have my commandments and keep them are those who love me; and those who love me will be loved by my Father, and I will love them and reveal myself to them."[7]

In Jesus' view, the commandments were realized through love. Jesus, therefore, offered his disciples and the Christian party a new commandment: "I give you a new commandment, that you [the disciples] love one another. Just as I have loved you, you also should love one another. By this everyone will know that you are my disciples, if you have love for one another."[8]

Love in Christianity begins with the love of God for Christ. "For God so loved the world that he gave his only Son, so that everyone who believes in him may not perish but may have eternal life."[9] In this view of things, God sent love, that is, his only Son, to save the world. "Indeed, God did not send the Son into the world to condemn the world, but in order that the world might be saved through him."[10]

Jesus, therefore, brought love to the center, and made it the core, of his religious perspective. "This is my commandment, that you love one another as I have loved you. No one has greater love than this, to lay down one's life for one's friends."[11] Jesus ceased to call his disciples servants and they could no longer call him master, because love meant the formation of an entirely new type of relationship.[12] Rather than servants or slaves, his disciples were, and they became, his friends, those whom he supported and loved and who supported and loved him.

Jesus' arrival at this point of view, that is, of basing his organization on love, constituted a real leap in human thought. Perhaps its time had come. Strong circumstantial evidence suggests, however, that Jesus might have obtained the concept from his father and mother.

Although Joseph was not his biological father, Joseph became Jesus' father by adopting him.[13] We sometimes neglect that God did not give Jesus only to Mary. God's angel visited both Mary and Joseph. While he was Mary's biological son, he was Joseph's son psychologically. Both were his parents and both loved him. It is probably from their love, and, as he deemed it, from the love of God, that he developed his view of love.

Knowing the love of his parents and the love of God, and having experienced love in his childhood, Jesus' psychology became a psychology based on love. From this psychology of love, Jesus brought the concept of love to the center of his Weltanschauung. He made love the essential condition for the realization of his platform. Basing his movement on love was more than a stroke of genius. It was one of the great practical achievements in human thought.

This platform of love, as the essential relationship between a person and God, constituted, of course, a break with Judaism. Judaism was, and it is, based on authority, on force, and on a compulsory relationship between the Jews and their God. Above all, as we have seen, the Jews are "to fear" Yahweh.[14] They have to "obey" Yahweh, their God.[15] "If you do not diligently observe all the words of this law that are written in this book, fearing this glorious and awesome name, [i.e., Yahweh] your God, then [Yahweh] will overwhelm both you and your offspring with severe and lasting afflictions and grievous and lasting maladies."[16]

Christianity, by way of contrast, is based exclusively on love. One follows the commandments because one loves others and loves God. In fact, for Jesus and his followers, *the* commandment is *to love*. As Jesus himself put it, "the Father himself loves you, because you have loved me and have believed that I came from God."[17] Jesus averred that God had loved him even before the foundation of the world.[18] Since God had loved him, and he loved God, Jesus believed that God sent his love, that is, he himself, into the world and thereby revealed that God "loved them [i.e., collective humanity as it comes to believe in Christ] even as you have loved me."[19]

Jesus did not believe, however, that his disciples should, nor that they could, love only themselves, their friends, and God. He pushed them and the concept of love to another stage: "You have heard that it was said, 'You shall love your neighbor and hate your enemy.' But I say to you, Love your enemies and pray for those who persecute you, so that you may be children of your Father in heaven."[20]

Anyone could return love and love those who loved them. A person who really loved, and especially if a disciple of Christ, loved even his and/or her enemies. Loving an enemy is difficult. But, if one loves, one will love even enemies. "If you love those who love you, what credit is that to you? For even sinners love those who love them. If you do good to those who do good to you, what credit is that to you? For even sinners do the same."[21]

Christ urged his followers to love their enemies. They were to do good to those who hated them. They should bless those who cursed them. And they should pray for those who abused them. "If anyone strikes you on the cheek, offer the other also; and from anyone who takes away your coat do not withhold even your shirt. Give to everyone who begs from you; and if anyone takes away your goods, do not ask for them again. Do to others as you would have them do to you."[22] In short, his followers were to forgive others their trespass, because the Father forgave them their trespasses.[23]

Christ brought out through his party the universal nature of love. "Love is patient; love is kind; love is not envious or boastful or arrogant or rude. It does not insist on its own way; it is not irritable or resentful; it does not rejoice in wrongdoing, but rejoices in the truth. It bears all things, believes all things, hopes all things, endures all things."[24]

One had to love others, one's father and mother, one's daughter and son, one's enemies and nature, and God.[25] " 'You shall love the Lord your God with all your heart, and with all your soul, and with all your mind.' This is the greatest and the first commandment. And a second is like it: 'You shall love your neighbor as yourself.' On these two commandments hang all the law and the prophets."[26] "For this is the message you have heard from the beginning, that we should love one another."[27]

The members of the Christian party came to believe that love came from God. Those who love are from God and en route to God. One knew God because of love since, in their view, God is, above all, a father. And, with one's mother, a father is par excellence the one we love. "God's love was revealed among us in this way: God sent his only Son into the world so that we might live through him. In this is love, not that we loved God but that he loved us and sent his Son to be the atoning sacrifice of our sins."[28] Since God loved them, necessarily, they reasoned, they had to love one another. By their mutual love and their love for God, and God's love for them, they would come to God, and as love, God would be perfected in them. "God is love, and those who abide in love abide in God, and God abides in them."[29]

Love would overcome fear. In love with one's parents, with nature, with others, and with God, one would not fear punishment. Thus, the Christians came to believe that Jesus was the Messiah and born of God. In loving God the Father, they necessarily had to love the son. As children of God, they themselves loved God and would, because of this love, obey his commandments. "For the love of God is this, that we obey his commandments. And his commandments are not burdensome, for whatever is born of God conquers the world."[30] For the Christians, therefore, the commandment, above all, is that they should love.[31]

Chapter 9

Jesus and Human Salvation

As expressed in the story of John the Baptist, Christ's followers believed that one could become righteous through baptism and confessing one's sins.[1] Christ then would baptize people "with the Holy Spirit and fire."[2] In other words, according to John the Baptist, the way to salvation was through the Messiah.[3]

Some humans would "be saved."[4] They would be saved once the son of God, as the Messiah, returned from heaven.[5] Apparently then, salvation would occur concomitantly with the formation of the kingdom of heaven.

All humans got into the kingdom of heaven. But, once in the kingdom, there would occur a separation of good from evil. Those who were into evil, and evil itself, would be plucked out. "The Son of Man will send his angels, and they will collect out of his kingdom all causes of sin and all evildoers."[6]

With the formation of the kingdom of heaven, or just prior to it, there would occur a catastrophic cosmic event. The sun would explode, or cease to burn, or some other planet or heavenly bodily would come and be for an extended time between the earth and the sun, or, more probably, dust particles thrown up by a nuclear war would block the sun and moon light, and even star light, from reaching the earth.[7]

At that moment, as sun, moon, and star light no longer reached the earth, the "sign of the Son of Man will appear in heaven" and everyone would see " 'the Son of Man coming on the clouds of heaven' with power and great glory."[8] The "Son of Man" would be accompanied by his angels.[9] The elected would then be separated from the damned.

At the start of the selection process, the Son of Man would say " 'Come, you that are blessed by my Father, inherit the kingdom prepared for you from the foundation of the world.' "[10] Those who have been "blessed" by God would inherit God's kingdom. All the others, together with Satan and Satan's angels, would be thrown into "the eternal fire prepared for the devil and his angels."[11]

Clearly then, according to Christ, the kingdom of heaven had been prepared before the birth of the world. Those who entered the kingdom of heaven would be those who have been "blessed by" God to inherit it.[12] The issue is, of course, a critical one: who, according to Christ, are those "blessed" by God?

Peter, one of the twelve in Christ's inner circle, thought that, as he understood it, that person would be saved "who fears [God] and does what is right."[13] Paul, in turn, believed that people could be turned from Satan to God and from sins to the forgiveness of their sins by their faith in Jesus Christ.[14] Thus, in Paul's view, one is saved by faith. " 'Everyone who calls on the name of the Lord shall be saved.' "[15] According to Paul, "if you confess with your lips that Jesus is Lord and believe in your heart that God raised him from the dead, you will be saved."[16] A person "is justified [i.e., will be saved] not by the works of the law but through faith in Jesus Christ."[17]

Jesus seemed to have believed that salvation was not procured exclusively either by faith or good work. Rather, it came by fulfillment of God's will. "Not everyone who says to me, 'Lord, Lord [i.e., who has faith in me],' will enter the kingdom of heaven, but only the one who does the will of my Father in heaven."[18] Humans have freedom of choice. Who then could be saved? "For mortals it is impossible, but for God all things are possible."[19]

Thus, in the final analysis, humans could not save themselves. God, and God alone, was the savior. "[T]o sit at my right hand and at my left [in heaven], this is not mine to grant, but it is for those for whom it has been prepared by my Father."[20] In trying to save themselves, humans could only follow Christ. After all, Jesus could influence God.[21] "Everyone therefore who acknowledges me before others, I also will acknowledge before my Father in heaven."[22] Thus, since humans had free will, God sent Jesus to earth " 'to save his people from their sins.' "[23] Jesus would influence God by giving "his life a ransom for many."[24]

Jesus believed that, by giving his life, he would augment his power because he would become what he was from the beginning: that is, a heavenly being. "For just as the Father has life in himself, so he has granted the Son also to have life in himself; and he has given him authority to execute judgment, because he is the Son of Man."[25] At the moment of the resurrection, therefore, "All authority in heaven and on earth [will have] been given to [Jesus]."[26] "Go therefore and make disciples of all nations," Jesus told his disciples. Baptize "them in the name of the Father and of the Son and of the Holy Spirit, and [teach] them to obey everything that I have commanded you."[27]

Clearly then, at the moment the Son of Man became the Son of God and was seated on the right hand of power, those from all nations who believed in him, and in his system, could, as he influenced God, become part and parcel of the elect.[28] "For God so loved the world that he gave his only Son, so that everyone who believes in him may not perish but may have eternal life."[29]

In the end, however, those saved would be "of the elect, whom he [i.e., God] chose."[30] Those saved would be, as elected, those who have done good, i.e., the righteous.[31]

Chapter 10

The Personality, Character, and Philosophy of Jesus of Nazareth

In reflecting over the long years to A.D. 29, before the fateful meeting with John the Baptist at the Jordan River, Jesus had reason to be satisfied. He had learned something about himself and his mission.

Jesus came extremely close to having been born, however, into a single-parent family. It took the hand of God, or a miracle, to avoid that fate. This miracle proved to be, however, the defining event in the formation of Jesus' personality.

The salient thing about Jesus then was his good fortune at birth. He was, and/or his parents believed him to be, a "child from the Holy Spirit."[1] His legal father, Joseph, was no child abuser, no alcoholic, no drug addict, no criminal, and not even a politician.

In about 6 B.C. however, Joseph was confronted with a complicated situation. His betrothed was found to be pregnant. If he had strictly followed Jewish law, Mary would have been exposed to grave danger. Under Jewish law, if she could not prove her virginity by means of a physical examination conducted by the elders of Nazareth, the "men of her town" were obliged to "stone her to death, because she [would] have been found guilty of] commit[ing] a disgraceful act in Israel by prostituting herself in her father's house."[2] We are told that Joseph's disinclination "to expose her to [this] public disgrace" stemmed from the fact that he was a "righteous man."[3]

51

Clearly, because we know that Joseph "found [Mary] to be with child from the Holy Spirit,"[4] the Lord's angel Gabriel visited Mary prior to, and not on the same night as, the angel's visit to Joseph's. Mary believed that, since she was a virgin, she could not have a baby.[5] The angel told her, however, that, " 'The Holy Spirit will come upon you, and the power of the Most High will over-shadow you; therefore the child to be born will be holy; he will be called Son of God.' "[6]

Mary seems to have given this explanation to an incredulous Joseph. Joseph hesitated to accept the theory of a virgin conception. He intended to "dismiss her quietly" in order to shield Mary from "public disgrace."[7] At that very moment, however, the Lord's angel "appeared to him in a dream."[8]

What the angel told Joseph shaped Jesus' life and has revolutionized the world. This is because millions upon millions believe, as did Jesus, that before there was Jesus, there was the Word. And the Word was as spoken to Joseph on that fateful night: " 'Joseph, son of David, do not be afraid to take Mary as your wife, for the child conceived in her is from the Holy Spirit. She will bear a son, and you are to name him Jesus, for he will save his people from their sins.' "[9]

The dream also changed Joseph's life. By implication, of course, it also saved Mary's life and that of the "child conceived in her."[10] Already reluctant to subject Mary to Jewish law, Joseph did as the angel of the Lord commanded him: he (1) took Mary as his wife and (2) adopted Jesus as his son. While in Bethlehem, he named his son and married Mary.[11]

It is far from certain that Mary and Jesus would have perished had Joseph dismissed Mary. After all, Joseph planned to do it in a way that would have avoided the application of Jewish law. But even if Mary had been put to trial before the elders of Nazareth, her death by stoning was far from certain because Mary might have won her case. The Nazareth elders might have decided for her on the basis of finding, during the physical examination, an intact hymen.[12] Whether Mary would have won her case is, however, a moot question. It is clear that, in her opinion, she remained a virgin.[13]

Jesus might well have been from the Holy Spirit. Joseph, in any event, accepted him as his own son. Thus, Jesus was quite fortunate. Strong circumstantial evidence suggests that Joseph was a loving father. Jesus could look, therefore, to the heavens, that is, to his father in heaven. But Jesus knew that his father on earth, since a loving father, was a model for, or modeled after, the father in heaven. The decisive thing about Jesus' mind and mental makeup then is his knowing a father's and a mother's love and his belief that, in addition to a loving father on earth, he had a loving father in heaven.

The salient thing about Jesus, therefore, was his family origin. Jesus could trace his ancestry back to God.[14] Jesus knew, moreover, that as the Son of God, he was supposed to be great. In fact, Gabriel, the angel, revealed the boy's mission to his mother: "He will be great, and will be called the Son of the Most High, and the Lord God will give to him the throne of his ancestor David. He will reign over the house of Jacob forever, and of his kingdom there will be no end."[15] In other words, as Joseph understood the boy's mission, the boy would "save his people from their sins."[16] Accordingly, Jesus came to view himself as a plenipotentiary from God. His mission was to divert evildoers to another path: the path of righteousness.[17]

As part of his mature world view, moreover, Jesus came to possess a theory of the universe. It is clear that he believed, of course, in God. Surprisingly, he also believed in the existence of Satan.[18]

There is no reason to believe that, as he formulated the new doctrine, Jesus discarded the Jewish view of Satan. According to the Jews, Satan was from heaven. "One day the heavenly beings [i.e., sons of God] came to present themselves before [Yahweh], and Satan also came among them."[19] As a Jew ethnically in the

Roman province of Galilee, Jesus seems to have accepted this point of view. At least we can find no evidence that he rejected it.[20]

In fact, Jesus believed that there were an earth and a heaven, with the devil, certain angels, and God "in heaven."[21] Jesus saw the world in motion: it was coming into being, but at the same time, it was going out of being. In Jesus' view, "heaven and earth [would] pass away."[22] Heaven was not on earth. It encompassed at least, however, the sun and the stars.[23] Heaven could and would be brought to the earth so that the earth and heaven would become one. Both would be, and they are, part of God's kingdom. The Kingdom of God seems to have been, therefore, a place on earth, or the earth was made into, and became part of, the Kingdom of God.[24]

Heaven was the seat or "the throne of God."[25] The earth was God's "footstool."[26] "Our Father [was, however,] in heaven."[27] God was "Lord of heaven and earth."[28] There existed, then, heaven, earth, and "outer darkness."[29] Moreover, there seems to have been another place, although in heaven, called "Paradise."[30]

Thus, in Jesus' view, humans could, and some would, populate each of these spheres of the cosmos at the proper time. Those who did not enter the kingdom of heaven would be "thrown into the outer darkness."[31] It is not clear where this might be, but, apparently, it is a place at a sufficient distance from the sun that the sun's light would not warm or even reach it.

Jesus spoke of hell as being situated "down" from heaven, suggesting thereby that hell was somewhere on, perhaps beneath, or within, the earth.[32] Closely associated with it was the devil or Satan.[33] Satan, the "tempter,"[34] was someone or something, and apparently a malevolent angel and/or Jesus' heavenly, but evil-inclined, brother,[35] offering power, wealth, and eternal life at one's command and without one having to be righteous.[36]

All the New Testament writers refer to an essential fact in Jesus' life: that he was the Messiah. He was also and essentially, they note, "the Son of God."[37] This belief or knowledge of his being the Son of God was the cardinal fact in shaping Jesus' Weltanschauung. In Jesus' view, God was omnipotent, omniscient, and perfect.[38] Some humans would come to know God. They had, however, to be righteous.[39] "Blessed are the pure in heart, for they will see God."[40]

Jesus' character, and indeed his whole life, was shaped by his preoccupation with the struggle against the devil.[41] Apparently, believing himself to be "the Lamb of God," Jesus thought that he was sent to extirpate "the sin of the world."[42] He believed that, since the righteous were already saved, he had come to earth "to call not the righteous but sinners."[43] He deemed his mission to be "to seek out and to save the lost," that is, those who were into evil and, therefore, those who followed, or were in the captivity of, Satan.[44]

Possessing this belief, and as part of his struggle to save sinners, Jesus wanted to confront directly and, although it was a most dangerous undertaking, to come vis-à-vis to the Jewish ecclesiastical establishment in Jerusalem.

Chapter 11

Jesus' Struggle with the Jewish Ecclesiastical Establishment and His Arrest

Once the disciples came to view him as the Messiah, and the son of God, Jesus planned a more direct confrontation with the Jewish religious establishment in Jerusalem. His disciples claim, after the fact of course, that Jesus foresaw the ultimate victory of his movement. "From that time on [i.e., from his founding an organization called the church], Jesus began to show his disciples that he must go to Jerusalem and undergo great suffering at the hands of the elders and chief priests and scribes, and be killed, and on the third day be raised."[1]

Jesus' strategy of confronting the Jewish ecclesiastical establishment directly in Jerusalem shook Peter and the disciples to the core. "God forbid it, Lord! This [i.e., being put to death] must never happen to you," said Peter.[2] Jesus, however, was adamant. Refusing to submit to being killed, while the human thing to do, meant submission to Satan rather than to the will of God. Jesus, therefore, told Peter, who opposed his strategy of confronting the Jewish ecclesiastical establishment in Jerusalem: "Get behind me, Satan! You are a stumbling block to me; for you are setting your mind not on divine things but on human things."[3]

Far better than his disciples, Jesus understood the political situation in Palestine. Palestine was then a colony, a principality, of

Rome. As such, although in the Middle East, it was part of, or annexed to, Europe. The Jewish religious establishment had certain, mainly ecclesiastical, powers in Jerusalem. Ultimately, however, especially in the secular, and particularly the political, realm, power in Jerusalem was vested in Rome and therefore in Pontius Pilate, Rome's governor.

Jesus was a *sui generis* figure in history, both charismatic and brilliant. He expected something electrifying to happen on the third day after his death, something so awesome as to shake Rome to its foundation. How it would occur, he did not say. The suggestion certainly seems to be, however, that it was planned before the fact.[4]

Jesus assumed that the Kingdom of God was just around the corner. "Truly I tell you, there are some standing here who will not taste death before they see the Son of Man coming in his kingdom."[5] Those who followed him, after he had been raised from the dead and seated on the throne of his glory, would "inherit eternal life."[6] As he admitted, however, it was beyond his power to guarantee to any of his followers a place in the Kingdom of God.[7]

While he seems to have wished to live,[8] Jesus reasoned that he was compelled to serve God. Accordingly, in the cosmic battle with Satan for the minds of men and women, he had "to give his life a ransom for many."[9] Jesus came to believe that Satan was so effective, or humans so sinful, that only by giving his own life could he rescue or have God rescue the sinful.

Life, therefore, was driving Jesus on to Jerusalem. His years in Galilee and the Judean countryside were history. He had come to another stage in his development.

At the Mount of Olives outside Jerusalem, Jesus did something assured of frightening the Jewish religious establishment. Knowing that, according to tradition, Israel's king was to arrive in Jerusalem, humble, and mounted on a donkey with a colt, Jesus had two of his disciples obtain use of a donkey and a colt from an individual in a small village near Jerusalem.[10] As Jesus sat on the donkey, a large crowd went before him spreading their cloaks and leafy palm tree branches on the road.[11] The impact electrified the crowd.

The crowds about him began shouting, "Hosanna [Praise be] to the Son of David! Blessed is the one who comes in the name of the Lord! Hosanna in the highest heaven!"[12] Still others shouted, "Blessed is the coming kingdom of our ancestor David!"[13] And the multitude of disciples, including the women who followed Christ, began to exclaim, "Blessed is the king who comes in the name of the Lord!"[14] And still others shouted, "Blessed is the one who comes in the name of the Lord—the King of Israel!"[15]

The whole thing had a colossal impact. All of Jerusalem seemed in turmoil. "Who is this?" some asked. Others answered, "This is the prophet Jesus from Nazareth in Galilee."[16] Thus, while the crowds were shouting that Jesus had the throne of David and came in the name of the Lord, the crowds bestowed upon Jesus the name that soon would become world famous: Jesus of Nazareth.

Jesus continued his great manifestation on reaching the temple in Jerusalem. He did something that probably occurred to him when he was a small boy. He drove out those who were selling and buying in the temple and he overturned the tables of the money changers and those who sold doves.[17] However, it was an act of defiance, and an assumption of power, calculated to bring Jesus tête-à-tête with the Jewish religious establishment. In fact, especially after hearing a multitude of children shouting, "Hosanna to the Son of David," the chief priests and the scribes became angry.[18] Even more, however, they were "afraid of him, because the whole crowd was spellbound by his teaching."[19]

On Monday morning, April 1, A.D. 30, Jesus returned to the city from Bethany where he and his entourage had spent the night.[20] As he had done the previous day, he taught in the temple. Certain of the chief priests and the elders of the people confronted him. They wanted to know who gave him the right to teach in the temple and to disrupt certain of its functions. "By whose authority are you doing these things, and who gave you this authority?"[21]

Jesus saw the question as it was intended to be, that is, as a trap. He skillfully maneuvered around the question and, in parables, explained that the tax collectors serving Rome and the prostitutes would have a better chance of entering the Kingdom of God than the Pharisees, scribes, and chief priests. "When the chief priests and the Pharisees heard his parables, they realized that he was speaking about them. They wanted to arrest him, but they feared the crowds, because [the multitude] regarded him as a prophet."[22]

The Jewish religious establishment had certain power, especially over matters in the temple. And so far as it was not opposed by certain sects, such as the Essenes, John the Baptist's followers, or the Christian party, the Jewish ecclesiastical establishment held power, in a religious sense, over the Jews in Palestine. But its power had limits. It could not, for example, arrest Jesus as long as he had the support of the masses.

The Pharisees, the major establishment party, sought therefore to provoke Jesus into challenging Roman power. Some of them, accompanied by some Roman officials, approached Jesus. The Pharisees posed a shrewd question, and thereby they hoped to reveal that Jesus was in rebellion against Rome's authority in Jerusalem. "Teacher," they began, "we know that you are sincere, and teach the way of God in accordance with truth, and show deference to no one; for you do not regard people with partiality. Tell us, then, what you think. Is it lawful to pay taxes to the emperor, or not?"[23]

Jesus knew their purpose. He had spent years in debate with the Pharisees. He understood that they were intending to entrap him so as to turn him over to Rome as a rebel against Roman power. Jesus made sure that his arrest would not be political, that is, based on opposition to Rome. He asked someone to show him a denarius, a Roman silver coin. Looking at the coin, Jesus asked, "Whose head is this, and whose title?"[24] The Pharisees answered, of course, "The emperor's." Jesus then exclaimed, "Give to the emperor the things that are the emperor's, and to God the things that are God's."[25]

Jesus' answer demonstrated his perspicacity. He explained that the people paid taxes to the emperor with the emperor's own money. Paying taxes to the emperor, therefore, had nothing at all to do with God.

The Pharisees, like the Christians, believed in the spirit, the existence of angels, and the resurrection. Their chief opponents, the Sadducees, did not believe in either. After Jesus smashed the Pharisees, the Sadducees took their turn in trying to entrap him. But, through his wisdom, Jesus silenced the Sadducees by showing that the Sadducees did not know that the Most High was God of the living rather than the dead.[26]

Jesus took his denunciation of the Pharisees and the scribes to his disciples and the crowds. He explained that the Pharisees and Sadducees did not practice what they preached.[27] They sought the best seats in the synagogues and the place of honor at banquets and sought to be seen by others. They wanted the multitude to call them rabbi, that is, teacher. Jesus explained, however, that the multitude were not to call the chief priests and scribes either rabbi or father "for you have one Father—the one in heaven" and "you have one instructor, the Messiah."[28]

In the ferocity of his attack on the Jewish religious establishment, Jesus excelled even John the Baptist. He called the scribes and Pharisees Satan's plenipotentiaries. "[W]oe to you, scribes and Pharisees, hypocrites! For you cross sea and land to make a single convert, and you make the new convert twice as much a child of hell as yourselves."[29] "You snakes, you brood of vipers! How can you escape being sentenced to hell?"[30]

From the viewpoint of the religious establishment, Jesus had become a dangerous man. Accordingly, Jesus warned his followers that the establishment would soon move more decisively against him as it became more assured of its sway over the multitude.[31] In fact, the religious establishment was plotting in Jerusalem at that very moment. The chief priests and the elders "gathered in the palace of the high priest, who was called Caiaphas, and they conspired to arrest Jesus by stealth and kill him."[32]

In its plot, the religious establishment was assisted of course by Judas Iscariot. Matthew suggests that Judas betrayed Christ into the hands of the religious establishment for "thirty pieces of silver."[33] That is not incorrect. However, it is not the whole of it as revealed by the fact that it was Judas who went to the chief priests and sounded them out by asking, "What will you give me if I betray him to you?"[34] His approaching them, rather than their having approached him, confirms that Judas first obtained the thought and the thirty pieces of silver were irrelevant except as a front to make the Jewish ecclesiastical establishment assume that he was betraying Christ for the money.

Luke and John offer the explanation, of course, that "Satan entered into him."[35] Their explanation is an admirable one, but it is only part of the reality. The best explanation seems to be that Judas may not have known Jesus' real perspective until the Christian party came to the Mount of Olives and Jesus commenced his final battle against the Jewish ecclesiastical establishment.

Jesus had warned his followers to "beware of the yeast [i.e., the teaching] of the Pharisees and Sadducees."[36] But, born in Judea, the only disciple from outside Galilee, Judas may really have been closer, in the final analysis, to the Jewish ecclesiastical establishment, and especially to the Sadducees, than to the Christian party. Moreover, sensing that he diverged from the Christian party on the question of the Messiah,[37] Judas may also have been troubled by an event at Simon's house in Bethany.

A woman came to Jesus in Simon's house and poured an extremely expensive ointment on Jesus' head as he sat at a table.[38] Judas Iscariot did not like what he saw. "Why was the ointment wasted in this way?" he asked. "For this ointment could have been sold for more than three hundred denarii, and the money given to the poor."[39] Jesus' use of the perfume in that way, since costly, was something that, as the party's treasurer and now in opposition to

Christ, Judas Iscariot could not tolerate. Whatever were the theoretical foundations for the split, it was this event that eventually revealed the break between Judas Iscariot and the Christian party.

The thirty pieces of silver just served as the pretext for the betrayal. Judas Iscariot would have done it in any case. John says that Jesus thought in fact that Judas Iscariot was "destined" to betray him.[40] Mark makes clear that it was the ointment episode that precipitated the split in the party. "Then [i.e., after witnessing the ointment episode] Judas Iscariot, who was one of the twelve, went to the chief priests in order to betray him to them. When they heard it, they were greatly pleased, and promised to give him money. So he began to look for an opportunity to betray him."[41]

The disciples are in agreement that Jesus knew that one of them would be lost in the final showdown with the Jewish religious establishment. "Truly I tell you, one of you will betray me."[42] It is clear that Judas Iscariot had decided before, or at least at the completion of, the Passover meal on Thursday evening, April 4, A.D. 30, to betray Christ. After the meal, the Christian party returned to the Mount of Olives. Judas Iscariot was not with them. Jesus suspected the reason. Being human and wanting to live but being also, as he believed, from the Holy Spirit and wanting to defeat Satan and to do the will of God, Jesus prayed that God should cause him to avoid being betrayed into the hands of sinners. "My Father, if it is possible, let this cup pass from me; yet not what I want but what you want."[43]

Jesus' hour, however, had come. Judas Iscariot arrived with a large police and military detachment sent by the chief priests and the elders. The group had swords and clubs. The armed party seized Jesus and arrested him. Peter drew his sword to, and he did, resist violently.[44] Jesus thought that violent resistance might, in its proper time, and even then only exceptionally, have its place. He could not see resisting violently, however, when the Scripture pointed to things happening as they were happening.[45]

Already sleepy from the long day and perhaps tipsy from the

wine at the Passover meal, the disciples fled to avoid being arrested. The Jewish temple police and the Roman soldiers "arrested Jesus and bound him."[46] It soon became apparent to Jesus that he was being led under guard to a certain place and for a particular reason.[47]

Chapter 12

The Trial and Execution of Jesus of Nazareth

After being arrested by the Jewish temple police and Roman soldiers, Jesus was taken to the home of Annas. Annas was the father-in-law of high priest Caiaphas. Annas "questioned Jesus about his disciples and about his teaching."[1] Clearly then, Annas' questions revealed what really troubled the Jewish ecclesiastical establishment: that is, the Christian party's doctrine.

Jesus disclaimed any secret doctrine. "I have spoken openly to the world; I have always taught in synagogues and in the temple, where all the Jews come together. I have said nothing in secret."[2] Annas saw that Jesus had spoken the truth and "sent him bound to Caiaphas the high priest."[3]

High priest Caiaphas had assembled the scribes and elders in his house late into the night.[4] Various witnesses came forward, and from the nature of the questions to the witnesses, Peter, one of the disciples, who observed the proceedings, reasoned that the Jewish high court, the Sanhedrin, or council, was looking for "false testimony against Jesus so that they might put him to death."[5] At least two of the witnesses testified that Jesus had said, "I am able to destroy the temple of God and to build it in three days."[6] It was obviously false testimony, and Jesus elected not to dignify it with a refutation.

The fraudulent nature of the testimony became obvious even to the council. The high priest, therefore, was compelled to exclaim to Jesus, "I put you under oath before the living God, tell us if you are the Messiah, the Son of God."[7] Jesus answered the first question, that is, whether he was the Messiah, by saying, "If I tell you, you will not believe; and if I question you, you will not answer. But from now on the Son of Man will be seated at the right hand of the power of God."[8] The high priest then, for the Sanhedrin generally, wanted Jesus to answer the second part of the question, by asking him, "Are you, then, the Son of God?"[9] Jesus replied in the affirmative: "You say that I am."[10]

On obtaining that answer, the high priest tore his clothes, "the custom of the judge who heard blasphemous words."[11] He exclaimed, "He has blasphemed! Why do we still need witnesses? You have now heard his blasphemy. What is your verdict?"[12] The Sanhedrin rendered its verdict. It found Jesus of Nazareth guilty.[13] And, at the punishment stage, it declared, "He deserves death."[14]

Although it met at night and its procedure might have been irregular, the Sanhedrin attempted to follow the rules by reconvening after dawn during the early morning. It then reconfirmed the verdict, formulated the indictment, and "bound Jesus, led him away, and handed him over to Pilate."[15] Whether the Sanhedrin strictly followed the rule is, in any event, unimportant. It is not to be expected that the rules would be strictly followed, especially in regard to such a dangerous opponent of the establishment as Jesus Christ. Defective trials are not all that uncommon even in an ancient or modern democracy.

It is obvious, however, that what happened at the high priest's house, and before the Sanhedrin, on Thursday night and apparently into Friday morning of April 5, A.D. 30, was the **trial** of Jesus Christ. The high priest had stated the charge, that is, the crime of blasphemy. And, of course, the verdict was the death penalty.

But, after the vote and to wrap an otherwise defective trial in a legal disguise, the Sanhedrin reconvened in the morning and formulated the indictment. The political reality in Jerusalem compelled the formulation of the indictment since only Rome could carry out the death penalty.[16] If Jesus were to be executed, it had to be in accordance with Roman law. Under Roman law, there was a right of appeal. A death sentence was automatically appealed to the Roman governor. However, since Jesus was not a Roman citizen, he himself did not have this right. It was the Sanhedrin that, paradoxically, had to appeal to the Roman governor to execute the sentence.

An indictment is the setting forth of the allegations against the accused. The Sanhedrin's indictment is extremely important, therefore, for understanding what occurred in Jerusalem on Friday, April 5, A.D. 30. The text of the Sanhedrin's indictment is well-known: *"We found this man perverting our nation, forbidding us to pay taxes to the emperor, and saying that he himself is the Messiah, a king."*[17]

The indictment was, in effect, in two parts, or there were two allegations. The first charge was *sedition*: we found this man perverting our nation by forbidding us to pay taxes to the emperor. The second charge was *blasphemy*: we found this man perverting our nation by saying that he himself is an anointed king. In other words, the indictment charged that Jesus was perverting the Jewish nation by his Christian doctrine. He had been perverting the Jewish nation through the propagation of his doctrine by urging Jews in Palestine not to pay taxes to Caesar and by attempting to convince the nation that he was the Messiah or Israel's anointed king. And a king on the throne in Jerusalem meant, ipso facto, less taxes to Caesar in Rome.

Pontius Pilate understood the indictment in precisely this way. He went immediately, therefore, to the heart of the matter and sought to establish whether the allegations were true. He asked Jesus, "Are you the king of the Jews?"[18] Jesus would not confirm that he did the things alleged because he believed himself the king of the Jews. Pontius Pilate saw immediately, therefore, that Jesus was not engaged in any sedition against Rome. He told the chief priests and the Sanhedrin delegation, "I find no basis for an accusa-

66

tion against this man."[19] Thus, the Roman governor, as the appellate court, reversed the conviction and acquitted Jesus of the offense.

The Sanhedrin, however, was insistent. They offered other evidence. "He stirs up the people by teaching throughout all Judea, from Galilee where he began even to this place."[20] At that moment, upon learning that he might be able to dispose of the appeal by disclaiming jurisdiction since Christ was from Galilee and Herod, the Roman official in control of Galilee, was temporarily visiting Jerusalem, Pilate sent Jesus "off to Herod."[21] Herod examined Jesus "at some length."[22] Like Pilate, Herod could not find any support in the evidence for the allegations. Herod, therefore, found Jesus not guilty and remanded him to Pontius Pilate.[23]

Pilate tried again to overrule the Sanhedrin. "You brought me this man as one who was perverting the people; and here I have examined him in your presence and have not found this man guilty of any of your charges against him. Neither has Herod, for he sent him back to us. Indeed, he has done nothing to deserve death. I will therefore have him flogged and release him."[24] Pilate, therefore, confirms our view: the Sanhedrin did not bring one charge; it brought several charges against Jesus.

The Jewish ecclesiastical leaders would not permit Pilate, however, to reverse the conviction. The Sanhedrin told Pilate that, "If this man were not a criminal, we would not have handed him over to you."[25] So Pilate tried another strategy: that is, he would refuse jurisdiction by returning the case to the Sanhedrin. "Take him yourselves and judge him according to your law."[26] The Sanhedrin pointed out that because its verdict was death, it would still be without jurisdiction. "We are not permitted to put anyone to death."[27]

Since the leaders of the Jewish religious establishment were so adamant, Pilate would have a second look. Perhaps he had missed something in finding the evidence insufficient to substantiate Christ's guilt. He asked Jesus again, "Are you the King of the Jews?"[28] Jesus responded, "Do you ask this on your own, or did others tell you about me?"[29] Pilate replied, "I am not a Jew, am I? Your own nation and the chief priests have handed you over to me. What have you done?"[30]

Christ explained, "My kingdom is not from this world. If my kingdom were from this world, my followers would be fighting to keep me from being handed over to the Jews. But as it is, my kingdom is not from here."[31]

Pilate wanted to dispense with the philosophy. "So you are a king?" Pilate asked.

"You say that I am a king," Jesus answered. "For this I was born, and for this I came into the world, to testify to the truth. Everyone who belongs to the truth listens to my voice."[32]

Pilate came to see that Jesus considered opposition to Rome to be irrelevant. Jesus had not come into the world to oppose Rome, but to reveal the nature, or the truth, of God.[33]

Pilate had no choice but to go back outside and inform the Sanhedrin of his decision. And in the process, he sought to find another way to release Jesus. He told the Sanhedrin and the crowds, "I find no case against him. But you have a custom that I release someone for you at the Passover. Do you want me to release for you the King of the Jews?"[34] The Sanhedrin shouted in reply that its members did not want Jesus released. They wanted instead a common bandit, a person who had been put in jail for insurrection against Rome and for murder, one Barabbas, to be released.[35]

Pilate still tried, however, to release Jesus by having him flogged.[36] His soldiers constructed a crown of thorns, put it on Jesus' head, and dressed him in a purple robe. Pilate then brought Jesus out in that outfit as he told the crowds, "Look, I am bringing him out to you to let you know that I find no case against him."[37]

The official religious leaders and the crowds yelled, however, "Crucify him! Crucify him!"[38]

Although a politician, Pilate attempted to be decisive. In fact, he told the members of Jerusalem's religious establishment, "Take him yourselves and crucify him; I find no case against him."[39]

The Sanhedrin was forced at that point to reveal its real reason for urging that Jesus be put to death. The allegation about sedition had been an attempt to persuade Rome of the necessity of the death penalty. Pilate, however, could not find sedition against Rome, and refused to do so. The Sanhedrin then told him, "We have a law, and according to that law he ought to die because he has claimed to be the Son of God."[40] Thus, within the crowd, the Sanhedrin and the Jewish police insisted that Pilate should, in effect, make the Jewish law proscribing death for blasphemy supreme to, or superimpose it on, Roman law. "Now when Pilate heard this, he was more afraid than ever."[41]

Pilate was confronted, therefore, with a new factor in the appeal. The Sanhedrin let it be known that if Pilate reversed the conviction, the Jewish religious establishment in Jerusalem would appeal to Caesar in Rome. They would say, in effect, that Pilate himself supported subversion and was, therefore, in opposition to, or at least no friend of, Caesar. "If you release this man, you are no friend of the emperor."[42]

Pilate tried to stand up even in the face of that threat. He brought Jesus out one last time, and said to the Sanhedrin and the crowds, "Here is your King!"[43]

The Sanhedrin and the crowds, however, cried out, "Away with him! Away with him! Crucify him!"

Pilate asked them one more time, almost pleading for their support, "Shall I crucify your King?"

The chief priests answered for the Sanhedrin and the crowds, "We have no king but the emperor."[44] That did it because the chief priests were telling Pilate that if he freed Jesus, Jesus and not Caesar would rule Jerusalem. At that point, Pilate "gave his verdict that their demand should be granted."[45] He "handed [Jesus] over to them [i.e., to a detachment of Roman soldiers] to be crucified."[46]

What happened, therefore, is that the Sanhedrin imposed the death penalty. Although Pontius Pilate did all that he could do consistent with his position to save Jesus, Rome carried out the execution.[47] Pilate's soldiers marched Jesus to Golgotha, the place of execution, as the women in the Christian party followed behind Jesus and wailed for him.[48]

The crucifixion occurred at about 9:00 A.M. on April 5, A.D. 30.[49] Four soldiers participated in the crucifixion.[50] While being attached to the cross, Jesus would not drink the wine and gall, a mixture that would have diminished his susceptibility to pain. He was hung from the cross as were two common criminals, one on each side of him. Shortly after 3:00 P.M., on that Friday, Jesus died.[51] Jesus' mother, his aunt, and many other women from his party witnessed the execution.

Pilate had an inscription written, in Hebrew, Latin, and Greek, and his soldiers attached it above Jesus' head on the cross. It read: "Jesus of Nazareth, the King of the Jews."[52] In Pilate's view, Jesus was crucified because he was the King of the Jews. Pilate shrewdly revealed that the crucifixion was for no offense, but that it occurred because the chief priests wanted the execution of Jesus. The chief priests, in turn, sought to have Pilate change the inscription to show an offense, that is, that Christ was crucified for a crime: "Do not write, 'The King of the Jews,' but, 'This man said, I am King of the Jews.' "[53] Pilate answered them, however, by saying, "What I have written I have written."[54]

Pilate thus revealed that Jesus was not executed for a crime, because the inscription over the cross repudiated the indictment. He was executed, instead, for being a king. Jesus' kingdom, as Pilate knew, however, was not of this world.[55] Circumstantial evidence suggests, therefore, that Christ lived to see the victory of the Christian doctrine over the Roman governor.[56] More than anything, it was the conversion of Pontius Pilate, the Roman governor, that compelled Jesus, at the moment of his death, to change his view about not sending a ministry to the Gentiles.

Chapter 13
Jesus and the Resurrection

Jesus had come a long way up that fateful day there in Jerusalem at about 3:00 P.M. on Friday, April 5, A.D. 30, when, at about age thirty-four, he rendered up his spirit to God and died on the cross. His reign on earth as the King of the Jews was history. His kingdom was yet to come if, as he believed, God's will be done.

Gone were the disputes with the Pharisees and Sadducees. They, and ostensibly not he, seemed to have won. There can be no doubt that he failed if his mission was to convert the Jews. The Jewish multitude went on their way, and Christ became but a footnote in Jewish history. There will be time enough in the future to consider, and for some to see, whether Jesus saved the Jews. In failing to convert the Jewish multitude, paradoxically, however, Jesus seems to have won because his followers converted the multitude in Europe.

Jesus knew, however, that he had failed. Converting the Jews from their ways and from sin was no easy task. Jesus, therefore, insisted that the Jews could be saved only if the Jewish ecclesiastical establishment in Jerusalem effectuated his death. In Jesus' view, he would have to undergo "great suffering at the hands of the elders and chief priests and scribes."[1] Because of his death, or despite it, however, "on the third day he [would] be raised."[2] Jesus clearly thought that he would die and be resurrected.[3] Ironically, however, he did not believe in the resurrection of the dead. Although the elect die, he observed, they are not dead, because it is the living who are

71

resurrected.[4] The Most High is the "God not of the dead, but of the living."[5]

According to Jesus, he would be "lifted up from the earth."[6] After that, and in due course, he would draw people after him into heaven. Those deserving it would obtain "eternal life."[7] But, before the elected could ascend into heaven, Jesus said that he would have to return to earth.[8] At his own resurrection, he would go "to the Father."[9] He was in the Father and the Father was in him.[10] "I am the way, and the truth, and the life. No one comes to the Father except through me. If you know me, you will know my Father also. From now on you do know him and have seen him."[11] His return to earth would be necessary to separate those "blessed" by God to "inherit the kingdom" from those destined forever to be with Satan.[12]

Jesus believed that, at his death, his spirit, in the form of the human spirit or the Holy Spirit, would light upon his disciples and those who sought to serve God. His disciples would no longer see him, except in spirit and in truth. In other words, Jesus anticipated that his death would facilitate the birth of Christianity. He held that, by his crucifixion and the resulting formation of the Christian religion, and as the son of God, he would conquer the world.[13] "Father, the hour has come; glorify your Son so that the Son may glorify you, since you have given him authority over all people, to give eternal life to all whom you have given him. And this is eternal life, that they may know you, the only true God, and Jesus Christ whom you have sent."[14]

Assuming that Jesus came from God, what, however, did Jesus do on earth? It is clear that Jesus created the Christian religion. But, ironically, he could create it, or he created it, only by his crucifixion, or rather his resurrection. As Jesus put it, "I have given them your [i.e., God's] word."[15] "As you have sent me into the world, so I have sent them into the world."[16]

Thus, in Jesus' view, the disciples had to go into the whole world. Although he had thought otherwise up to his trial, proclaiming the gospel solely to the Jews was not the sum of it. One of the great mysteries then is how, at his trial and crucifixion, Jesus communicated this message to his disciples. The disciples have offered the explanation that Jesus conveyed the new strategy to them after his death but during the resurrection.[17]

We have seen that the basis for the new strategy came to Jesus on his meeting Pontius Pilate. It may well have been on the cross that he saw his error. In any event, the disciples have him saying before ascending into heaven, "All authority in heaven and on earth has been given to me. Go therefore and make disciples of all nations, baptizing them in the name of the Father and of the Son and of the Holy Spirit, and teaching them to obey everything that I have commanded you."[18]

The disciples were to proclaim the message: that is, the gospel, or the good news, of Jesus Christ. Jesus told them that repentance and forgiveness of sins were to be "proclaimed in his name to all nations, beginning from Jerusalem."[19] "The one who believes and is baptized will be saved; but the one who does not believe will be condemned."[20] "Blessed are those who have not seen and yet have come to believe."[21]

The evidence confirms that Jesus *died* on the cross.[22] The Jewish establishment wanted his body and the bodies of the two criminals removed before sundown. Accordingly, Joseph of Arimathea, one of Jesus' clandestine disciples, went to Pilate requesting permission to remove Jesus' body.[23] Pilate gave that permission. Jesus' body, therefore, came into the possession of his disciple. As Jesus' follower and a member of the Sanhedrin, Joseph had not agreed to the death penalty.[24]

Many of Jesus' followers, including many of the women who had come up with him from Galilee, had observed Jesus being entombed. His disciples had intended to bury Jesus in accordance with the burial custom of the Jews.[25] They put his body temporarily in a new tomb in a garden near where he had been crucified and left the area in obedience to the Jewish sabbath.[26]

Something, however, had happened by Sunday, April 7, A.D. 30. Jesus' official disciples could not find his body. Some of the women returned to the tomb and found the stone had been rolled from it.[27] Mary Magdalene suspected what had happened: "They have taken the Lord out of the tomb, and we do not know where they have laid him."[28] Like Moses' burial place,[29] no one knows to this day where Jesus' burial place happens to be. His body has been lost to the ages.

Mary Magdalene and several other of Jesus' female followers were met, in a vision or in actuality, by two men near the tomb. What these men told the women is extremely important: "Why do you look for the living among the dead? He is not here, but has risen. Remember how he told you, while he was still in Galilee, that the Son of Man must be handed over to sinners, and be crucified, and on the third day rise again."[30]

The two men were not angels. Their familiarity with Jesus' doctrine reveals, in a circumstantial way, their identity. They were, as was Joseph of Arimathea, part of Christ's clandestine followers. They had revealed that Jesus was dead but that, in spirit and truth, he had risen. "Then they [the women] remembered his words, and returning from the tomb, they told all this to the eleven [since Judas Iscariot had committed suicide] and to all the rest."[31]

The remaining eleven disciples did not, of course, believe the story. They deemed the talk about the resurrection of Jesus to be "an idle tale."[32] Mary Magdalene and the other women, however, believed that Jesus was alive and their belief infected the eleven disciples.[33] Two of the disciples, Peter and John, were greatly surprised by the turn of events. On hearing Mary Magdalene's story, they took off running to the tomb.[34] They did not, of course, find the body of Christ.

The official disciples had not comprehended what Jesus had told them: that is, that he "must rise from the dead."[35] What happened to Jesus' body colossally impacted them. The clue to what happened to Jesus' body is revealed through Mary Magdalene who, somewhat later, looked into the tomb.[36] Mary Magdalene thought that she saw, and she may have seen, as she viewed it, two angels sitting where Jesus had been lying, one at his head and the other at his feet.

What Mary Magdalene told the angels is crucial evidence for understanding what happened to Jesus' body: "They [i.e., the secret disciples] have taken away my Lord, and I do not know where they have laid him."[37] As she turned, she saw a person who she thought was Jesus. "[B]ut she did not know that it was Jesus."[38] She assumed the man to have been the gardener. Her comment reveals, of course, her thinking. And her perspective points to what happened to Jesus' body: "Sir, if you have carried him away, tell me where you have laid him, and I will take him away."[39]

Clearly, therefore, the clandestine disciples had taken Jesus' body. However, as revealed by Mary Magdalene, if the clandestine disciples had not removed the body, the official Christian party, the eleven disciples and Jesus' Galilee entourage, would have taken the body and buried it.

The Jewish ecclesiastical establishment was just as surprised by the turn of events as the eleven disciples. The chief priests and the Pharisees from the Jewish establishment expected the eleven disciples and the official Christian party to steal Jesus' body and say that Jesus had risen.[40] Moreover, they saw something else: that, as they understood Jesus' doctrine, the resurrection of Christ was becoming, or it would become for Christ's followers, an essential article of faith.

Once the Jewish establishment learned that Jesus' body was not in the tomb, some of its leaders bribed the Roman soldiers to say that Jesus' disciples, the official Christian party, " 'came by night and stole him away while we were asleep.' "[41] That, however, was not the reality. The eleven disciples and Jesus' Galilee entourage were as surprised as the Jewish establishment.

The eleven disciples took it literally that Jesus had risen from the dead because they could not find his body. They eventually seemed to see Jesus withdrawing from them and being carried into heaven.[42] They also commenced to worship Jesus as, in effect, God.[43] They came to view Jesus as being, in fact, God since, as the Son, he was from the Father.

Jesus' followers finally had come to understand Jesus' point of view. As Jesus expressed it, "the Messiah is to suffer and to rise from the dead on the third day, and that repentance and forgiveness of sins is to be proclaimed in his name to all nations, beginning from Jerusalem."[44] Once the eleven disciples understood Christ's doctrine, the religion of Christianity, as the doctrine of Jesus Christ, finally burst into being.

Chapter 14

Jesus Christ and the Origin of Christianity

Although an impressive and brilliant individual, Jesus of Nazareth became world historic because of the revolution in religion occasioned by his formation of a new view of the nature of God. God became essentially a loving God, a father who protected, and was calling home, his children. While Christianity developed out of Judaism, it was a step beyond Judaism. It was not the consummation of Judaism, but an altogether different religion.

Jesus grew up Jewish in Palestine. As he taught and proclaimed the good news of the coming of the kingdom of God in its cities and villages, he came to understand that the Jewish multitude were not going to follow him. He "began to reproach the cities in which most of his deeds of power had been done, because they did not repent."[1]

The Christian party, or at least Jesus, never intended to take the message to the Gentiles. Ironically, however, Jesus Christ and his disciples had their most astonishing impact in the cities of Tyre and Sidon, i.e., in Lebanon among the Gentiles, rather than in such Jewish cities as Chorazin, Bethsaida, and Capernaum.[2]

Jesus and his party drew large crowds among the Jews in Galilee and in Jerusalem on his final visit to the city. But the Christians never won the Jewish people.

An incursion into Lebanon surprised Jesus by the strength of his support, however, amongst the Gentiles. Matthew tells what happened: "Just then a Canaanite [i.e., Palestinian] woman from that region came out and started shouting, 'Have mercy on me, Lord, Son of David; my daughter is tormented by a demon.' "[3] Jesus, however, would not help her in her struggle to retrieve her daughter's mind from Satan's control. As he explained, "I was sent only to the lost sheep of the house of Israel."[4]

Clearly then, Jesus had not escaped his upbringing as a Jew. He still thought that it was his mission to save the Jews and not all the peoples of the world. What happened next, however, revealed the weakness in Jesus' view of his doctrine as a Jewish religion. At the same time, it highlighted the strength of Jesus' doctrine: that is, that, while it would not win the Jewish multitude, it could win the Gentiles.

We have, therefore, this early example of the astonishing success that Christianity would have on those in Europe. After all, Palestine was then, although in the Middle East, Western European territory. Even Jerusalem was controlled, at least politically, from Rome. It is an essential fact, therefore, that Christianity originated as a **European** religion although it originated in Palestine.

Jesus refused to help the Palestinian. The Palestinian woman, however, was adamant. She came and knelt before him, saying, "Lord, help me." Jesus told her, however, that, "It is not fair to take the children's food [i.e., to use the heavenly power intended for the Jews] and throw it to the dogs [i.e., to use the power on behalf of the Palestinians]."[5]

The Palestinian's answer was so insightful, and so profound, that Jesus could not turn her away, "Yes, Lord, yet even dogs eat the crumbs that fall from their masters' table."[6] In other words, as she saw it, even though certain Jews might consider her inferior, dogs and masters shared a common reality since they ate of the same food. It is extremely important, therefore, to note that, as he viewed it, Jesus utilized the power intended for the Jews to save this Palestinian woman's daughter. Matthew reveals what Jesus said and what happened: " 'Woman, great is your faith! Let it be done for you as you wish.' And her daughter was healed instantly."[7]

Jesus had instructed his disciples to take the message only to the Jews in and about Palestine. "Go nowhere among the Gentiles, and enter no town of the Samaritans, but go rather to the lost sheep of the house of Israel."[8] Although Jesus and the Christians recruited among the Jews, few joined the Christian party. Christianity has not succeeded to this day in converting the Jews. The Jewish multitude considered Jesus to be another Jewish prophet. Support for this can be seen in the way the crowds reacted to him as he entered Jerusalem on April 1, A.D. 30. The comments of the crowds about him in Jerusalem revealed their view of him: "This is the prophet Jesus from Nazareth in Galilee."[9]

Clearly then, the Jews viewed Jesus as a "prophet" whereas the Gentiles, as we have seen, viewed him as the "Lord." The Jews who became Jesus' disciples grew up amongst the Gentiles and had, as did Christ, Palestinian Aramaic as their native language. His only follower from Judea, Judas Iscariot, whose native language was Hebrew, finally rejected the doctrine and betrayed Jesus to the Jewish ecclesiastical establishment. Those who were receptive to the new doctrine were those who had contact with the Christian party but who were not Jewish: the Syro-Phoenician woman, Pontius Pilate, his wife, the Roman soldiers, and one of the criminals whose ethnicity, however, is unknown although he is presumed to have been Jewish.[10]

As he could understand Jesus' perspective, Pontius Pilate was thrilled by it. Although he considered Jesus to be a king, Pilate still attempted, as we have seen, to release Jesus. It seems to have been the Gentiles and those Jews who were influenced by their absorption of, or their integration into, Gentile culture who were receptive to, and fascinated by, Jesus' teachings. Jesus, however, at least up to April 5, A.D. 30, considered himself to have been a **Jewish** prophet and the Messiah of the Jews rather than a human prophet and the Messiah of the world.

Jesus was proving more Essenic and most Jewish. He did not seem to comprehend that his doctrine was a break with Judaism, although he believed it a break with official Judaism. He was actually preaching Christianity as a form of Judaism. This may explain why the Pharisees, the Sadducees, and the high priests met him with such hostility. Jesus thought that he was the true exponent of Judaism. The Pharisees, the Sadducees, and the high priests were, he believed, preaching something other than the truth. Jesus, therefore, warned his followers to beware of "the teaching of the Pharisees and Sadducees."[11]

Jesus was trying to substitute Christianity into the shell of Judaism. Although originating in Essenic Judaism and in the Roman Empire, Christianity was never the continuation of Judaism. Nor was it a return to Judaism or its essence in a new form. Christ's doctrine, however, was a manifestation of the Essenic point of view and specifically the continuation of John the Baptist's doctrine beyond, however, John the Baptist.

Jesus was not always aware of that fact. He was thrown back, therefore, on a few disciples and several clandestine proponents of the party's doctrine. These disciples and their converts would later build the organization into a church. What Jesus did not do, because it was not then his view of his mission, was to build the Christian organization, the church, primarily amongst the Gentiles in Palestine.

The strategy of taking Christianity into Europe occurred to Jesus at some point on or about April 5, A.D. 30. His disciples claimed to have seen Jesus, at least in their vision, in Galilee some weeks after his death. Matthew says that Jesus, then, told them to go into all nations in the recruitment of sinners to the church. The sinners were to be baptized and, in the process, they would accept the Christian doctrine of God as the Most High revealed as "the Father and . . . the Son and . . . the Holy Spirit."[12] That was the standpoint of the Christian party beyond Jesus although, it is true, Jesus seems to have come to the new strategy during his trial and at his execution. Somehow he communicated the strategy to his followers, or at least they came to the strategy during the period of the resurrection.[13]

Luke says that the eleven disciples thought they were seeing a ghost there in Jerusalem some days, or for even some weeks, after Christ had been crucified.[14] It was at this point that Jesus is said to have "opened their minds to understand the scriptures."[15] What the disciples did or what Jesus did acting on the minds of the disciples was, as they assert, to add a correction to the Christian party's doctrine. Although it had its seeds in Jesus' earlier point of view, the new approach came too late for Christ. The disciples were told the new approach: "Go into all the world and proclaim the good news to the whole creation."[16]

Something radical happened, therefore, to the Christian organization there in Jerusalem in April of A.D. 30. Jesus and the Christian party finally concluded that Jesus had come to save not just the Jews, nor simply even all humans, but, as with Noah, the whole of God's creation. And Jesus finally had revealed God to be, or he returned to the view of God as, in Genesis, a universal God, the God of all creation.

Christianity has several stages to its formation. We know something about the first stage: that is, that the new doctrine was, for a time, interlocked with the perspective of John the Baptist. The explanation for this seems to be that Jesus' mother was related to John the Baptist. And as his relative, Christ's mother was probably also an Essene. His legal father, Joseph, was a righteous man and the Son of David. Properly read, the gospel is telling us that Joseph was mainstream Jewish.

But even Joseph was coming under the influence of the Essenic Judaism developing at a distance from Jerusalem and there in and about Galilee. This is proved by the fact that, after discovering Mary to have been pregnant, Joseph would not permit the application of Jewish law. He "planned [therefore] to dismiss her quietly."[17] The extent to which Joseph came under the influence of

Mary, and therefore that the Jesus home in Galilee was Essenic, is not clear. What is clear is that Jesus' sisters married mainstream Jews. But his brothers, James, Joseph, Judas, and Simon,[18] and his mother joined the Christian party.

We might say then that Jesus came to his point of view because his parents, in teaching him about God, taught him that his mission was that of saving Israel. That certainly was the opinion of his mother's relatives. Elizabeth said, for example, that God was, in fact, Yahweh. And, as the Jewish God, Yahweh sent Jesus to help "his servant Israel, in remembrance of his mercy, according to the promise he made to our ancestors, to Abraham and to his descendants forever."[19] Jesus was to be, in Elizabeth's and Zechariah's view, a "mighty savior for us in the house of his servant David."[20]

As Joseph remembered it, the Lord's angel told him that Mary would bear "a son, and you are to name him Jesus, for [i.e., because] he will save his people from their sins."[21] The word Jesus or *Yeshua* in Hebrew, Joseph's native tongue, is the syncopated variant of *Yehoshua* or "God is help."[22] Since from God, Jesus was an aid, or some help, in humanity's struggle for righteousness and therefore for its liberation from Satan's influence or control.

As Jesus, Joseph seems to have deemed the expression, "he will save his people from their sins,"[23] to have conveyed the thought that Jesus would save the Jews. But perhaps Joseph and Jesus interpreted the words "his people" too narrowly. Gabriel seems to have explained God's plan of a virgin conception in more detail to Mary:

> Do not be afraid, Mary, for you have found favor with God. And now, you will conceive in your womb and bear a son, and you will name him Jesus. He will be great, and will be called the Son of the Most High, and the Lord God will give to him the throne of his ancestor David. He will reign over the house of Jacob forever, and of his kingdom there will be no end.[24]

The expression "of his kingdom there will be no end" cannot

mean that on "the throne of his ancestor David," i.e., as King of the Jews, Jesus would have no limit to his kingdom. Rather, what is meant is that as "the Son of the Most High" his kingdom would include everyone and everything. All things in fact must eventually come into, and become part of, God's kingdom. Thus, in brief, Jesus' mission was to save his people. But since all humans are capable of becoming children of God, Christ's people are those who become righteous in the sight of God.

Proof for this point of view is not difficult. The proper interpretation of Jesus' mission was revealed when Mary and Joseph took the boy to Jerusalem shortly after his birth. Simeon, a righteous man, was there. He had been preserved by the Holy Spirit to a ripe old age. "It had been revealed to him by the Holy Spirit that he would not see death before he had seen the Lord's Messiah."[25] The Holy Spirit directed Simeon toward Joseph and Mary with baby Jesus. Simeon took Jesus into his arms and praised God: "Master, now you are dismissing your servant in peace, according to your word; for my eyes have seen your salvation, which you have prepared in the presence of all peoples, a light for revelation to the Gentiles and for glory to your people Israel."[26]

Thus, according to Simeon, Jesus was to save *all* peoples. Jews could be proud of him because, after all, as the founder of Christianity, he was ethnically Jewish. However, Jesus' mission was to take the message of salvation to Jews and Gentiles alike.

However it happened, then, that the eleven disciples arrived at that conclusion, they returned Christianity to what it was in the beginning. Before or shortly after Christ's birth, as elucidated by the Lord's angel and revealed by Simeon under the guidance of the Holy Spirit, embryonic Christianity held that the way to salvation is through, or it would be revealed by, the "light" because it was Jesus' mission to reveal the nature of God to *all* the people of the earth.

It was not until after the death of Christ, or during the resurrection, however, that Christianity was officially founded. Before that point, Jesus had been *building* Christianity through the instrumentality of the Christian party.

Simeon had revealed God's real plan to Jesus' parents. The baby's "father and mother were amazed at what was being said about him."[27] Jesus thought, however, that his true aim was to save the Jews. He was trying to substitute his doctrine into the shell of Judaism. He had spent more than thirty years developing his point of view before commencing to do God's work. And, after being baptized and refining his doctrine, he further developed it there at his trial and on the cross.

As he shared, or was about to share, the totality of the human experience, Jesus cried out in a loud voice: "*Eloi, Eloi, lema sabachthani?*"[28] This Aramaic expression is said to mean, "My God, my God, why have you forsaken me?"[29] Jesus' cry was a prayer, despite his illusions about saving all Jews and his hitherto insufficient knowledge of the nature of God, for redemption.[30]

Jesus had failed in his supposed mission of bringing the Jews to God by way of Christianity. Before dying, however, he came to a new realization of his mission. It was then that, reflecting on his defeat, Jesus learned that his mission was not to convert exclusively the Jews. He had, he realized, failed in that. In spite of that failure, however, as a human, Jesus asked God to redeem him.

After his resurrection, his disciples claimed, Jesus was other than human. He now went to, and became part of, God. There were now three powers revealed to be, or denominated, God. These were said to be, as revealed by Gabriel to Mary and by Jesus Christ to his disciples, the Father, the Son, and the Holy Spirit. And the Holy Spirit was, of course, God's power or, in brief, as expressed in its essence, love.[31]

John made the point explicitly: "In the beginning was the Word, and the Word was with God, and the Word was God. He was in the beginning with God."[32] Thus, in the Christian religion, Jesus was from the Holy Spirit, and the Holy Spirit is the power of God.

As the creation of God, Jesus was, however, special: the son of God and, therefore, the Word of God.[33]

Christianity became a world historic religious perspective because, by becoming the major religion in many parts of the world, it is the story of how, as the Christians argue, Jesus Christ came from and later returned to God by means of the Holy Spirit.

As a human, his disciples aver, Jesus of Nazareth was redeemed by God[34] because, of course, he was the Son of God. His disciples then came to worship him since they worshiped God.[35] Jesus, however, was not God. He was, they say, the light of God, that is, the heavenly being who, born as Mary's son, enabled humans to know God.[36] In the Christian religion, Jesus Christ became, and he is, the means through which all people may receive the Holy Spirit and therefore the love of God.[37]

It was when the disciples understood all of this that, as developed by Jesus Christ and predicated on free will, love, and a universal God, Christianity became the new convenant and in time the dominant religion in the Roman Empire.

Notes

Chapter 1: Birth

1. *The Holy Bible, Containing the Old and New Testaments with the Apocryphal/Deuterocanonical Books: New Revised Standard Version* (Nashville, 1989), Matt. 1:1–17. (References below to the books of the Old and New Testaments are to this volume.)

   A short note about the primary and secondary sources: The secondary literature on Jesus is bountiful, but it is highly speculative. My study is based on a reliable source. For the most part, it is based on the primary source, that is, the reflections of Jesus' mother and his disciples and/or their beliefs about Jesus as reflected in the New Testament. After all, "[p]ractically everything that is known about Jesus comes from the four Gospels in the New Testament." *See Jesus and His Times,* edited by Kaari Ward (Pleasantville, 1987), p. 7; and A. E. Harvey, *Jesus and the Constraints of History* (Philadelphia, 1982), p. 1.

   It has been argued, of course, that the "Gospel account of Jesus in the New Testament is not an objective representation of events." *See* R. Joseph, Hoffman, *Jesus Outside the Gospels* (New York, 1984), p. 7.

   Clearly, however, the New Testament elucidates a history of events as revealed in and through the testimony of the participants, including those who remembered Christ's teachings. The New Testament is, therefore, an excellent source for revealing the life of Jesus and his teachings. *See* Acts 1:1, where Luke says that in his Gospel, he "wrote about all that Jesus did and taught."

   If one is to find the essence of Christianity and reveal its origin, one surely cannot find it except where it happens to be; that is, in the New Testament. The latter then is the primary source for a study of Christianity. By basing the present study on facts, and ferreting out Jesus' and his party's beliefs, I have hoped to avoid, and certainly have aimed not to add to, "the present disenchantment with the modern quest of the historical Jesus." James P. Mackey,

Jesus, the Man and the Myth: A Contemporary Christology (New York and Ramsey, 1979), p. 12.

2. Certain scholars assume it to have been the reverse: that is, that Matthew, *see* Matt. 1:1–16, described the genealogy of Joseph. *See* James E. Talmage, *Jesus the Christ: A Study of the Messiah and His Mission According to Holy Scriptures both Ancient and Modern* (Salt Lake City, 1961), p. 86; James B. Bell, *The Roots of Jesus: A Genealogical Investigation*, ed. by Richard I. Abrams (Garden City, 1983), pp. 15 and 48; and Michel Gasnier, *Joseph the Silent*, trans. by Jane Wayne Saul (New York, 1962), p. 21. From the structure of the New Testament, however, it can be argued that Matthew delineates the genealogy of Mary.

3. Matt. 1:16.

4. Luke 3:23.

5. Matt. 1:17.

6. Matt. 1:1.

7. Luke 1:27, 3:31.

8. Matt. 1:20.

9. Luke 1:32–33; *see* Talmage, *Jesus the Christ*, pp. 86–87; and Bell, *The Roots of Jesus*, p. 15.

10. Luke 3:38, 4:3; Gen. 1:26–27, 2:7.

11. John 1:1, 14.

12. Matt. 1:20–21, 24–25; Luke 3:23, 38; Gen. 1:26–27.

13. Luke 1:27.

14. Luke 1:56.

15. Matt. 1:18.

16. Matt. 1:25. Early Jewish tradition seems to suggest that the father is to name the son. *See* Gen. 5:3, 28–29 and Luke 1:13. Thus, by naming Jesus, Joseph, in effect, adopted Jesus as his son.

17. Matt. 1:18.

18. Matt. 1:19.

19. Deut. 22:23.

20. Tob. 12:15. *But see* Mark 13:32, where Jesus confirmed that there were "angels in heaven." He said that there were, however, "more than twelve legions of angels." Matt. 26:53. In ancient Rome, a legion numbered up to seven hundred men in the cavalry and six thousand men in infantry.

21. Matt. 1:24.

22. Matt. 1:20–21.

23. Matt. 1:24–25.

24. Matt. 1:25.

25. Luke 1:35.

26. *See* R. D. Rucker, *Eros and the Sexual Revolution: Studies in the Psychology of the Human Mind* (New York, 1991), pp. 50–51. Even Jesus, although said to be the "Son of God," *see* Luke 1:35, was born, as all humans are born, of woman so that life, even for him, was not created anew because it was perpetuated through Mary.

27. Matt. 1:18.

28. Luke 1:26–27.

29. Luke 1:36.

30. Luke 1:18.

31. Luke 1:13.

32. Luke 1:22.

33. Luke 1:17, 13, 76.

34. Luke 1:36.

35. Luke 1:38.

36. John 1:1, 14.

37. Luke 1:5.

38. Luke 1:26, 36.

39. Luke 1:35.

40. Luke 1:39.

41. Luke 1:56.

42. Luke 2:4.

Chapter 2: Childhood

1. Luke 2:1–2.

2. Luke 2:3.

3. Luke 2:4.

4. Matt. 1:24.

5. Matt. 1:25.

6. Luke 2:5.

7. Luke 2:6–7; Matt. 1:24–25; *see* C. Milo Connick, *Jesus: The Man, the Mission, and the Message* (Englewood Cliffs, 1974), pp. 111–112.

8. *See* Michael Grant, *Jesus: An Historian's Review of the Gospels* (New York, 1977), pp. 9 and 171, who argues that Jesus "probably" was born in "Nazareth in Galilee." The proof shows, however, that shepherds near Bethlehem found Jesus, as a small baby, "in the manger" in Bethlehem, and it is the boy's mother's testimony that he was born in Bethlehem. Luke 2:19. A mother's

testimony about her son's birthplace cannot be overcome by speculation and surmise.

9. Luke 2:7.
10. Matt. 1:16.
11. Matt. 1:25.
12. Luke 2:7. (Emphasis added.)
13. Matt. 12:47, 13:55.
14. Matt. 13:56, 12:50.
15. John 19:25; Luke 1:56.
16. Luke 1:36, 39.
17. Luke 1:43.
18. Luke 1:69.
19. Luke 1:76.
20. Luke 2:8–11.
21. Luke 2:16, 18.
22. Luke 2:19.
23. Luke 2:21.
24. Matt. 2:1.
25. Matt. 2:2.
26. Matt. 2:16.
27. Matt. 2:11.
28. Matt. 2:16.
29. Matt. 2:11.
30. Ibid.
31. Ibid. (Emphasis added.)
32. Matt. 2:2.
33. Matt. 2:3.
34. Matt. 2:4.
35. Matt. 2:6.
36. Matt. 2:12.
37. Luke 2:22.
38. Lev. 12:4, 6.
39. Luke 2:22, 27.
40. Luke 2:29–32.
41. Luke 2:32.
42. Luke 2:33.
43. Luke 2:34–35.
44. Luke 2:36–38.
45. Luke 2:39.
46. Matt. 2:13.

47. Ibid.
48. Matt. 2:15.
49. Matt. 2:20.
50. Matt. 2:16.
51. Matt. 2:19–20.
52. Matt. 2:22.
53. Matt. 2:23.
54. Ibid.

Chapter 3: Youth

1. Luke 2:39.
2. *See* Luke 2:42. The sense of what Luke is saying confirms that Jesus' probable birth was in the winter since he was twelve at Passover.
3. Luke 2:41.
4. Luke 2:40.
5. Luke 2:41–42.
6. Luke 2:51.
7. Luke 2:40.
8. Luke 2:44.
9. Mark 6:3; John 7:3–5; Matt. 12:46–50, 13:55–56.
10. Luke 2:43.
11. Luke 2:44.
12. Ibid.
13. Luke 2:48.
14. Luke 2:46. The best interpretation of this is that, after having searched for Jesus, on the day spent going from and on the day spent returning to Jerusalem, his parents found him in the temple on the third day of their search. *See* Luke 2:44–46. After all, the search started, we are told, on the first day. *See* Luke 2:44.
15. Luke 2:48.
16. Luke 2:49.
17. Luke 2:50.
18. Luke 2:47–49.
19. Luke 2:46.
20. Luke 2:47.
21. Luke 2:51.
22. Luke 2:52.

23. Ibid.
24. Luke 2:51–52.
25. Luke 3:1.
26. Luke 3:23. (Emphasis added.)
27. Matt. 3:13.
28. Matt. 3:14.
29. Ibid.
30. Matt. 3:15.
31. Luke 1:76.
32. Matt. 3:16–17.

Chapter 4: Jesus and John the Baptist

1. Luke 1:13.
2. Luke 1:7.
3. Luke 1:6.
4. Luke 1:19.
5. Luke 1:13–17.
6. Luke 1:36.
7. Luke 1:40.
8. Luke 1:41.
9. Luke 1:43.
10. Luke 1:76–77.
11. Luke 1:80.
12. Matt. 3:2.
13. Matt. 3:5–6.
14. Matt. 3:3.
15. Matt. 3:4.
16. Matt. 3:5–6.
17. Matt. 3:7–10.
18. Matt. 3:10.
19. Matt. 3:11.
20. Luke 3:16.
21. Luke 1:77.
22. John 1:10–13.
23. John 3:27–29.
24. John 1:34.
25. Luke 1:16–17.

26. *See* Friedrich Schleiermacher, *The Life of Jesus*, ed. with an introduction by Jack C. Verheyden, trans. by S. Machean Gilmour (Philadelphia, 1975), p. 259, who notes that: "John the Baptist was a man of the old covenant and remained so, even though he proclaimed something new that was at hand."

27. Matt. 11:10.

28. John 1:29.

29. Luke 1:68–79.

30. John 1:29–34, 3:27–29.

31. Matt. 11:2–6.

Chapter 5: Becoming Jesus Christ

1. Matt. 3:13; Mark 1:9.

2. Luke 3:22.

3. John 1:32–34.

4. Luke 3:23.

5. Luke 4:1.

6. Luke 2:52.

7. Luke 4:3.

8. Matt. 4:4.

9. Luke 4:9–11.

10. Luke 4:12.

11. Luke 4:5.

12. Luke 4:6.

13. Matt. 4:9.

14. Matt. 4:10.

15. John 1:28.

16. John 1:25.

17. John 1:26–27; Matt. 3:11–12.

18. John 1:29–31.

19. John 1:34.

20. John 1:37.

21. John 1:41.

22. Mark 1:19–20.

23. John 2:11.

24. Mark 1:34.

25. John 1:49.

26. John 1:51.

27. Matt. 4:23–25.
28. Mark 1:39.
29. Luke 4:18–19 (emphasis added); *see* Isa. 61:1–2.
30. Luke 4:21.
31. Luke 4:23–30.
32. Matt. 14:3–11.
33. Mark 1:14.

Chapter 6: Jesus' View of God

1. Matt. 1:1; Luke 3:38.
2. Gen. 11:27–28.
3. Jth. 5:8.
4. Ibid.
5. Gen. 11:27–28.
6. G. W. F. Hegel, "The Spirit of Christianity and Its Fate" (1798–1799), *Early Theological Writings*, trans. by T. M. Knox, with an introduction, and fragments translated by Richard Kroner (Philadelphia, 1971), pp. 185–186.
7. Gen. 25:7.
8. Gen. 11:30.
9. Gen. 12:1–4.
10. Gen. 12:5–7.
11. Gen. 12:6.
12. Gen. 12:7.
13. Jth. 5:9.
14. Gen. 13:14–18.
15. Exod. 3:8, 23:31; 1 Kings 4:21–24; Deut. 1:7; Gen. 15:18–21.
16. Gen. 17:1.
17. Gen. 17:8.
18. Ibid.
19. Gen. 17:7.
20. Gen. 17:12–14.
21. Exod. 2:11–14.
22. Exod. 3:7.
23. Exod. 3:8.
24. Exod. 23:31; Deut. 1:7; Gen. 15:18–21.
25. Exod. 3:14.
26. Exod. 3:15.

27. Exod. 3:18.
28. Exod. 23:13.
29. Exod. 6:3.
30. Exod. 5:1.
31. Exod. 5:3.
32. Gen. 1:1–3, 9, 11.
33. Gen. 1:4.
34. Gen. 1:27.
35. Gen. 5:1.
36. Gen. 1:28.
37. Gen. 2:8.
38. Gen. 2:10.
39. Gen. 2:14.
40. Gen. 2:17.
41. Gen. 3:14.
42. Gen. 3:16.
43. Gen. 3:17–19.
44. Gen. 6:5–7.
45. Gen. 6:9–19, 7:13, 21.
46. Exod. 34:13–14.
47. Gen. 9:4.
48. Gen. 9:11.
49. Jth. 5:8.
50. Deut. 14:1–2.
51. Deut. 3:5–7, 1:7–8, 2:31–34.
52. Gen. 17:8.
53. Exod. 20:2.
54. Lev. 18:4.
55. Gen. 17:7.
56. Deut. 10:14–15.
57. Exod. 6:7.
58. Exod. 29:45–46.
59. Deut. 6:4.
60. Lev. 22:33.
61. 2 Sam. 7:22, 23.
62. 2 Sam. 7:24.
63. 2 Sam. 22:32.
64. Luke 3:23.
65. Luke 2:52.
66. Matt. 10:5–7.

67. Matt. 15:21.
68. Matt. 15:22.
69. Matt. 15:24.
70. Matt. 15:22.
71. Matt. 15:28.
72. Matt. 16:12.
73. John 10:16.
74. Matt. 2:2.
75. Matt. 21:46.
76. John 8:39–59.
77. John 1:17–18; *see* Matt. 5:17–20.
78. Luke 24:46–49; Mark 16:15–18; Matt. 28:18–20.
79. At the beginning, even before Jesus was born, it was revealed that God was the Father, the Son, and the Holy Spirit. As the Angel Gabriel told Mary in revealing how she would become pregnant, "The *Holy Spirit* will come upon you, and the power of the *Most High* will overshadow you; therefore the child to be born will be holy; he will be called *Son* of God." *See* Luke 1:35 (emphasis added). At the end of his journey on earth as Jesus Christ, Jesus had arrived at exactly that point of view. *See, infra,* chapter 14, pp. 82–85.
80. Gen. 1:1; *see* Matt. 28:18–20.
81. John 1:17.
82. *See* Hegel, "The Spirit of Christianity and Its Fate," *Early Theological Writings, supra,* p. 253, who notes that: "To the Jewish idea of God as their Lord and Governor, Jesus opposes a relationship of God to men like that of a father to his children."

Chapter 7: Jesus and the Kingdom of God on Earth

1. Matt. 4:23.
2. Luke 8:1.
3. Matt. 4:25.
4. Mark 1:14; Matt. 11:5.
5. Mark 1:38.
6. Mark 1:39.
7. Matt. 4:17.
8. Mark 1:14.
9. Matt. 5:3.
10. Matt. 5:6.

11. Matt. 5:8.
12. Matt. 5:3–10.
13. Matt. 5:9.
14. Matt. 5:17–20.
15. Matt. 6:10.
16. Matt. 6:13.
17. Matt. 9:12–13.
18. Matt. 10:7.
19. Matt. 16:28.
20. Matt. 13:24–30.
21. Matt. 13:31–32.
22. Matt. 13:41–43.
23. Matt. 13:47–48.
24. Mark 10:27.
25. Matt. 22:13–14; John 3:13–21.
26. Matt. 20:23.
27. Matt. 24:14; Luke 24:47.
28. Matt. 24:5–8, 11–14.
29. Matt. 24:36.
30. Matt. 24:44.
31. Matt. 25:13, 24:42.
32. Matt. 25:46.
33. Luke 17:21.

Chapter 8: The Role of Love in Jesus' Perspective

1. *See* Rucker, *Eros and the Sexual Revolution.*
2. Exod. 20:2–17.
3. Deut. 6:5.
4. Deut. 30:16–20.
5. Deut. 6:13.
6. Deut. 6:18.
7. John 14:21, 23–24.
8. John 13:34–35.
9. John 3:16.
10. John 3:17.
11. John 15:12–13.
12. John 15:15.

13. Matt. 1:21–25.
14. Deut. 31:12; *see* Bamber Gascoigne, *The Christians* (New York, 1977), p. 14.
15. Deut. 28:1.
16. Deut. 28:58.
17. John 16:27.
18. John 17:24.
19. John 17:23.
20. Matt. 5:43–45.
21. Luke 6:32–33.
22. Luke 6:29–31.
23. Matt. 6:14–15.
24. 1 Cor. 13:4–7.
25. Matt. 10:37.
26. Matt. 22:37–40.
27. 1 John 3:11.
28. 1 John 4:9–12.
29. 1 John 4:16. On the transference of love from one generation to the next, *see* R. D. Rucker, *Drugs, Drug Addiction, and Drug Dealing: The Origin and Nature of, and the Solution to, the American Drug Problem* (New York, 1991), p. 52.
30. 1 John 5:3–4.
31. 2 John 1:5–6.

Chapter 9: Jesus and Human Salvation

1. Matt. 3:6, 13–17.
2. Matt. 3:11.
3. Matt. 3:12.
4. Matt. 10:22.
5. Matt. 10:23.
6. Matt. 13:41, 49.
7. Matt. 24:29.
8. Matt. 24:30.
9. Matt. 25:31.
10. Matt. 25:34.
11. Matt. 25:41.
12. Matt. 25:34.
13. Acts 10:35.

14. Acts 26:18.
15. Rom. 10:13.
16. Rom. 10:9.
17. Gal. 2:16.
18. Matt. 7:21.
19. Matt. 19:26.
20. Matt. 20:23.
21. Matt. 19:28–29.
22. Matt. 10:32.
23. Matt. 1:21.
24. Matt. 20:28.
25. John 5:26–27.
26. Matt. 28:18; John 5:21–24.
27. Matt. 28:19–20.
28. Mark 16:16; John 3:15, 17–21.
29. John 3:16.
30. Mark 13:20, 27.
31. John 5:29; Matt. 13:43, 49–50.

Chapter 10: The Personality, Character, and Philosophy of Jesus of Nazareth

1. Matt. 1:18.
2. Deut. 22:20–21.
3. Matt. 1:19.
4. Matt. 1:18.
5. Luke 1:34.
6. Luke 1:35.
7. Matt. 1:19.
8. Matt. 1:20.
9. Matt. 1:20–21.
10. Matt. 1:20.
11. Luke 2:5–7, 21, 27; Matt. 1:24–25.
12. Deut. 22:15, 17.
13. Luke 1:34; Matt. 1:23.
14. Luke 3:23–38.
15. Luke 1:32–33.
16. Matt. 1:21.

17. Matt. 5:17–20; Mark 16:15–18.
18. Matt. 4:10.
19. Job 1:6.
20. Luke 10:17–18; Matt. 25:41.
21. Matt. 6:9–10, 13, 24:31; Luke 10:18.
22. Matt. 5:18.
23. Matt. 24:29–30.
24. Luke 17:21.
25. Matt. 5:34.
26. Matt. 5:35.
27. Matt. 6:9.
28. Matt. 11:25.
29. Matt. 8:12.
30. Luke 23:43.
31. Matt. 8:12.
32. Matt. 11:23.
33. Matt. 4:1, 8, 10–11.
34. Matt. 4:3.
35. *See* Job 1:6–12; Matt. 4:1–11; Mark 1:11, 13; Luke 4:2–13; but compare John 1:14, 3:16.
36. Matt. 4:3–10; Luke 4:2–13.
37. Mark 1:1; Luke 3:38; John 1:18; Matt. 3:17.
38. Matt. 6:8, 5:48.
39. Matt. 5:10.
40. Matt. 5:8.
41. 1 John 3:8.
42. John 1:29.
43. Matt. 9:13.
44. Luke 19:10; Matt. 13:37–43.

Chapter 11: Jesus' Struggle with the Jewish Ecclesiastical Establishment and His Arrest

1. Matt. 16:21.
2. Matt. 16:22.
3. Matt. 16:23.
4. Matt. 20:18–19.
5. Matt. 16:28.

6. Matt. 19:28–29.
7. Matt. 20:23.
8. Matt. 26:38–46.
9. Matt. 20:28; 1 John 3:8.
10. Matt. 21:2–5.
11. Matt. 21:7–8.
12. Matt. 21:9.
13. Mark 11:10.
14. Luke 19:38.
15. John 12:13.
16. Matt. 21:11.
17. Matt. 21:12–13; Luke 19:45–46.
18. Matt. 21:15.
19. Mark 11:18.
20. Matt. 21:17–18.
21. Matt. 21:23.
22. Matt. 21:45–46.
23. Matt. 22:16–17.
24. Mark 12:16.
25. Mark 12:17; Luke 20:25.
26. Matt. 22:32.
27. Matt. 23:2–3.
28. Matt. 23:6–10.
29. Matt. 23:15.
30. Matt. 23:33.
31. Matt. 26:2.
32. Matt. 26:3–4.
33. Matt. 26:15.
34. Ibid.; Mark 14:10–11.
35. John 13:27, 30; Luke 22:3–6.
36. Matt. 16:6.
37. John 13:12–21.
38. Matt. 26:6–7.
39. Mark 14:4–5; John 12:5–6.
40. John 17:12.
41. Mark 14:10–11.
42. Matt. 26:21.
43. Matt. 26:39.
44. John 18:10; Matt. 26:51.
45. Matt. 26:52–56; John 18:36.

46. John 18:12, 3; Mark 14:43; Luke 22:4, 52.
47. John 18:13.

Chapter 12: The Trial and Execution of Jesus of Nazareth

1. John 18:19.
2. John 18:20–21.
3. John 18:22–24.
4. Matt. 26:57.
5. Matt. 26:59.
6. Matt. 26:61.
7. Matt. 26:63.
8. Luke 22:67–69.
9. Luke 22:70.
10. Ibid.; *see* Mark 14:62.
11. Joseph Klausner, *Jesus of Nazareth: His Life, Times, and Teaching*, trans. by Herbert Danby (New York, 1925), p. 343.
12. Matt. 26:65–66.
13. Mark 14:64.
14. Matt. 26:66.
15. Mark 15:1.
16. George M. Lamsa, *The Man from Galilee: A Life of Jesus* (Garden City, 1970), pp. 269 and 270.
17. Luke 23:2. (Emphasis added.)
18. Luke 23:3.
19. Luke 23:4.
20. Luke 23:5.
21. Luke 23:7.
22. Luke 23:9.
23. Luke 23:11.
24. Luke 23:14–16.
25. John 18:30.
26. John 18:31.
27. Ibid.
28. John 18:33.
29. John 18:34.
30. John 18:35.

31. John 18:36.

32. John 18:37.

33. Clearly, Jesus' fight was against evil and/or Satan. As David Winter, *The Search for the Real Jesus* (Wilton, 1982), p. 91, notes, "The revolution he urged . . . was not the overthrow of the social order but the transformation of the human heart." *But see* Hyam Maccoby, *Revolution in Judaea: Jesus and the Jewish Resistance* (New York, 1973), p. 195, who asserts that: "As a Jew, [Jesus] fought not against some metaphysical evil but against Rome." *See* 1 John 3:8.

34. John 18:38–39.

35. John 18:40; Luke 23:19.

36. John 19:1.

37. John 19:4.

38. John 19:6.

39. Ibid.

40. John 19:7.

41. John 19:8.

42. John 19:12.

43. John 19:14.

44. John 19:15.

45. Luke 23:24.

46. John 19:16.

47. Shusaku Endo, *A Life of Jesus*, trans. by Richard A. Schuchert (New York, Ramsey, and Toronto, 1978), p. 139, notes that "Rome recognized the residual right of the Sanhedrin to pass a sentence of death but reserved to itself the right to execute such sentences."

48. Luke 23:27.

49. Mark 15:25; Matt. 27:45.

50. John 19:23.

51. Mark 15:34.

52. John 19:19.

53. John 19:21.

54. John 19:22.

55. John 18:36.

56. *See* John 18:33–40, 19:7–15. Pilate's change of position can be seen in the fact that he ceased to call Jesus "this man" and started calling him a "king." *See* John 18:29, 39. Although Pilate knew Christ to be a king, and a king with a kingdom in heaven, Pilate still thought being a king was no crime and wanted to release Christ.

Chapter 13: Jesus and the Resurrection

1. Matt. 16:21.
2. Matt. 20:19.
3. Matt. 17:23.
4. Luke 20:38; John 11:25.
5. Matt. 22:32.
6. John 12:32.
7. John 12:50.
8. John 14:3.
9. John 14:12.
10. John 14:10–11.
11. John 14:6–7.
12. Matt. 25:31–34, 46, 24:30–31.
13. John 16:33.
14. John 17:1–4.
15. John 17:14.
16. John 17:18.
17. Mark 16:14–15.
18. Matt. 28:18–20.
19. Luke 24:47.
20. Mark 16:16–17.
21. John 20:29.
22. *See* Winter, *The Search for the Real Jesus*, pp. 109–110; *but see The Historical Jesus: A Scholarly View of the Man and His World*, ed. by Gaalyah Cornfeld (New York, 1982), p. 187.
23. John 19:38.
24. Luke 23:50–54.
25. John 19:40.
26. Luke 23:54–56.
27. Luke 24:2–3.
28. John 20:2.
29. Deut. 34:6.
30. Luke 24:5–7.
31. Luke 24:8–9.
32. Luke 24:11.
33. Luke 24:19–24, 34.
34. John 20:3–4.
35. John 20:9.

36. John 20:11.
37. John 20:13.
38. John 20:14.
39. John 20:15.
40. Matt. 27:63–64.
41. Matt. 28:13, 15.
42. Luke 24:50–51.
43. Luke 24:52; Matt. 28:17.
44. Luke 24:46–47.

Chapter 14: Jesus Christ and the Origin of Christianity

1. Matt. 11:20.
2. Matt. 11:21–23.
3. Matt. 15:22.
4. Matt. 15:24.
5. Matt. 15:25–26.
6. Matt. 15:27.
7. Matt. 15:28.
8. Matt. 10:5–6.
9. Matt. 21:11.
10. Luke 23:39–42, 47.
11. Matt. 16:12.
12. Matt. 28:19.
13. Acts 1:2. Luke says that Christ caused the disciples to have visions and/or dreams and, in this way, by causing them to believe him to be alive, *see* Acts 1:3, Christ gave "instructions through the Holy Spirit to the apostles whom he had chosen." *See* Acts 1:2.
14. Luke 24:37.
15. Luke 24:45.
16. Mark 16:15.
17. Matt. 1:19.
18. Mark 6:3.
19. Luke 1:54–55.
20. Luke 1:69.
21. Matt. 1:21.
22. *See Webster's Unabridged Dictionary of the English Language* (New York, 1989), p. 766.

23. Matt. 1:21.
24. Luke 1:30–33.
25. Luke 2:26.
26. Luke 2:29–32.
27. Luke 2:33.
28. Mark 15:34.
29. Matt. 27:46.
30. Ps. 22:1–31.
31. Matt. 28:19.
32. John 1:1.
33. Luke 1:35; Matt. 1:20.
34. Luke 23:46; John 19:30; Ps. 31:5.
35. Luke 24:52–53.
36. John 1:9.
37. John 1:29; 3:16–17, 8:42, 17:26.

Index